The Pro Se Guide to Legal Research & Writing

By Raymond E. Lumsden

"Education makes a people easy to lead, but difficult to drive; easy to govern, but impossible to enslave". – Lord Henry Brougham

"You cannot run away from a weakness; you must sometimes fight it out or perish. And if so, why not now, and where you are?" – Robert Louis Stevenson

Freebird Publishers
www.FreebirdPublishers.com

Freebird Publishers

Box 541, North Dighton, MA 02764
Info@FreebirdPublishers.com
www.FreebirdPublishers.com

Copyright © 2020
The Pro Se Guide to Legal Research & Writing
By Raymond E. Lumsden

All Freebird Publishers titles, imprints, and distributed lines are available at special quantity discounts for bulk purchases for sales promotions, premiums, fundraising, educational, or institutional use.

ISBN-13: 978-1-952159-08-4

Printed in the United States of America

Foreword

It was once said long ago that a person could teach Japanese to a chimpanzee, if we could somehow relate the subject matter to them. Of course, we now know that statement to be true, since we have been able to teach chimpanzees how to use sign language, obey our instructions, etc.

Effective legal writing entails part of the very same conclusion. In order to effectively communicate the facts and conclusions to our intended audience, we must write in a way that best relates to the reader. For the purposes of this book, the readers are judges who are unable to grant the relief you are seeking if they cannot understand your argument.

It's no secret as to how terrible most lawyers write and how badly most all prison "writ writers" and pro se inmates write. In fact, the very term "legal writing" has come to be synonymous with poor writing, with all its verbosity, legal prose and jargon. That is why most all states have made it illegal to use legal jargon and require plain English writing.

I have attempted to make this book different than all the other books, articles and manuals related to legal writing, largely due to my intended target audience, inmates. Despite my extensive legal training and persuasive writing expertise and in order to relate the subject matter to my intended audience, I must take it back to the "old school" known as English class. The reason for this is twofold:

- Plain English is the required and most effective writing style
- Most inmates have a limited writing understanding or education

What I intend to do is teach to you how judges read legal documents in true fashion, what impacts them and what obtains the best outcome. Whether it's a legal letter, memorandum, brief or motion, it's imperative that it be written properly and effectively.

My hope is that after reading this book, you are better versed and equipped to advance your claims and more importantly, to win.

– Raymond E. Lumsden

Table of Contents

Chapter One: The Writing Process

Writing any type of legal document takes time, consideration and real planning. The writing process most taught in law school has three stages that prove to be best effective: (1) prewriting, (2) drafting and (3) revising and editing the material.

Following these stages is the best and most assured way to better get your intended message across to your reader. While each of these stages is extremely important and should receive your utmost attention, the prewriting stage should receive most of your time and effort. You may find it necessary to draft and revise your writing multiple times in order to produce the best work. Let's look at each stage of the process so that you are better able to understand them and how they will benefit your writing.

Prewriting Stage

As I previously indicated above, this is the first step in the writing process. During this stage of the process you will be conducting your necessary research, devising your outline/plan of what you want to write. Clarity, understanding and accuracy are the most important aspects of effective legal writing and will produce the best work, therefore, the best results.

You should begin the prewriting stage by making the determination of who you are writing to, your target audience. You need to determine the purpose of the legal writing, its importance and what you wish to then accomplish with the writing/document. Things to ask yourself at this stage of the process are: (1) Who will be reading it and (2) What background do you know about the person(s) who will be reading it?

Is it a clerk, a lawyer or a judge? It's imperative that you know because each of those people requires a different tone and approach in your style and direction of writing. I'll address that a little later in the book.

You should also be thinking about the type of legal document you will be writing. Is it a legal letter, a motion, a memorandum or a brief? What is it that you wish to accomplish with your writing, and what do you want the reader to think or do regarding the legal document?

What is your time frame or deadline? How long should it be, and what is the required format? Remember, legal writing requires a very distinct style and structure than traditional writing. Organization is vital to the legal document being interpreted clearly and obtaining the understanding of the intended reader.

Next, you need to gather the intended research and facts that you wish to put into your writings. Creating an outline helps keep the information and research organized so that it flows as you write it. Creating an outline in the prewriting stage will be extremely helpful to you by keeping your brain focused and your ideas in order. This will save you a lot of time and energy.

Of course, the type of legal document you are writing will determine the correct outline you should create and what it looks like. You should be sure to include the facts, issues, points and assertions that you want to include in your document to give you the best chance of success.

Once the outline is created, be certain that it's specific to the facts, the intended audience and that its "flows" for the reader. A good outline will look something like this:

I.   Trial counsel has a duty to seek out expert witnesses to assist with the defense.
    (A)   The Supreme Court settled this issue in *Ake v. Oklahoma* (1985).
    (B)   In the case of an indigent client, counsel has an obligation to request funds from the court on behalf of his client.
    (C)   An expert witness could have assisted counsel in explaining complicated facts related to forensic evidence, therefore affecting the outcome of the trial.
II.   Trial counsel was ineffective for failing to seek out and obtain an expert witness.

As I indicated in my book, *The Habeas Corpus Manual*, a popular way to produce a good outline is to use the "whirlybird" method taught in a lot of paralegal and law schools.

You begin by drawing the outline of the whirlybird and give it a name or title in the middle. From that point, you simply create branches then sub-branches that support your ideas. There is no right way or wrong way; it's simply meant to get your ideas down so that you can later make better sense of them, therefore organizing them.

There need not be a right, left, bottom or top to your whirlybird. It doesn't matter where you write, what or if it will make it to your final outline. This method is simply for brainstorming your thoughts and ideas.

When you are finished, the information you will need is right there in front of you, and all you will need to do next is organize it all. An example of a completed whirlybird may look something like the drawing I've provided on the next page.

As you can see from my example, the title of my whirlybird was related to the issue of Ineffective Assistance of Counsel (IAC). From there, I simply allowed my thoughts to "run", becoming organized according to the right argument. Consequently, I can better organize these thoughts and ideas into my outline that will be used for the legal document. I promise you, if you use the whirlybird method, it will greatly impact your organization, detail and persuasive writing. You will need all of these to successfully accomplish what you want to in your writings.

One of the biggest struggles with legal writing is writer's block. It can be difficult trying to find a starting point, determining how to say what you want to say, etc. The whirlybird eliminates writer's block and encourages you to brainstorm, identify the points you want to make and present the facts most likely to bring you relief.

Drafting

This is the second stage of the legal writing process and will best be done in a quiet, relaxing place where you can focus without distraction. Concentration is the key to the required creativity during this very important stage of the process. Here is where you are most likely to experience writer's block, which happens to the best of writers. I advise you to begin your drafting immediately after you've completed the prewriting of your document so that the subject matter is fresh in your mind.

The information and research you gathered during the prewriting stage will now be used in your first draft. This is also where your outline will be helpful in assisting your creativity and writing. When writing your first draft, be sure to follow the format as well as the organizational style of the type of document you are drafting. More importantly, keep in the forefront of your mind the audience and purpose of the document you are writing.

Writing a good, clear and concise document requires more than one draft usually, until you become a more effective writer. This will happen with time and with the writing of multiple drafts and documents. We will get into what and how to write the draft further in the book, so don't get worried just yet. The sole purpose at this point is simply to familiarize you with the writing process and what each stage requires. The ins and outs, dos and don'ts, will be addressed in detail further into the book.

Effective legal writing isn't a simple task; there is a lot to learn and remember. This is why lawyers charge such high fees. It's also why law schools, and paralegal schools, spend so much time and focus on legal writing.

Revising and Editing

At this stage, you will make appropriate revisions, corrections and edits. You are focused on correcting and improving your work, paying very particular attention to the formatting and organization. This will make the document professional, clear and precise.

Again, as you did in the drafting, be certain to make sure the document is tailored to the right audience intended. Make sure your message is clear and understandable to the reader. Remove any unnecessary words and be certain that the words you use are forceful and persuading. Again, we will get further into that later in the book.

You will likely need to edit your writing multiple times, trying to detect grammatical errors, typos and misspellings. Having a dictionary or thesaurus handy will be of great benefit to you at this point. Keep in mind that while computer programs are helpful, they don't successfully identify incorrect words. For example, if you accidentally typed the word "decent" when you intended to type "descent", the spell checker would not identify the mistake. People are still better editors than computers.

If you have someone you can trust to read the documents, it often helps to locate mistakes that you missed. Two sets of eyes are always better than one. And besides, if you don't have access to a computer at your prison even the best spell-checking software won't help you. So, it is all settled...use a dictionary or thesaurus when editing.

In my training and experience, it helps to read the document aloud so you will be able to make certain it is clear and error free. Reading it out loud, word by word, will help you identify missing words or awkward sentences. In fact, if someone will read it out loud to you, that's even better. As the final step in this process, wait one day and read the final draft one more time. If it does not make sense to you...it won't make any sense to a judge, clerk, lawyer or anyone else either.

The main point of writing a legal document is, of course, to effectively communicate information and facts. Therefore, it's vital that your work is accurate and makes sense. Writing well will guarantee that readers will receive the right message, come to your intended conclusion and hopefully do what you want them to do. I mean, isn't that the whole point? Proper grammar, spelling, punctuation, tone, style and content are vital in effective legal writing.

Legal Citations

In most legal documents, letters, reports, memorandums, briefs, etc., you will usually be required to include information from laws, statutes and other legal authorities and records to support your statements and arguments.

When you make reference to these various sources, you must cite them. These all require strict forms that you must follow so that your intended reader can understand and relate to them. Think of legal citations as a form of language if you will. Everyone should be using the same language so that everyone is communicating with and understanding each other. It would not do anybody any good if a person were speaking Japanese, while another was speaking German. If you want your intended reader to understand, and more importantly agree with you, then you have to speak to them in the same "language".

Where there are numerous sources of legal citation manuals, be certain to use the citation manuals that your reader(s) understand or use. Once you begin, be certain to continue using the same source throughout the legal document as to avoid miscommunication.

The information included in legal citations tends to vary, especially in prison law libraries, as opposed to the "outside" legal community. That being said, most all legal citations have the following parts:

- Title
- Author
- Location
- Year of publication

In addition to the above, some may also include other information which may be formatted differently. Be sure to choose a style and format at the beginning of your legal writing and stick with it throughout. If you alternate between styles in your legal writing you will certainly mix your messages, thus losing the attention and following of your audience.

Also, and most importantly...prior to beginning your legal writing, be sure to check with your local court to determine their rules related to legal formatting and citations. Most courts will have their own rules, and failure to follow these rules will make your legal writing worthless no matter how wonderful, convincing and persuasive it may be.

Here I will break down some of the various citation rules you may wish to follow, which are common in the legal industry everywhere.

Short Citations

Once you have cited a case with full citation, you aren't required to use the full citation moving forward. This, in my opinion, is one of the biggest mistakes inmates and pro se legal writers make. It tends to make the writing multiplicative, long and needlessly repetitive.

For instance, when you cite a legal source for a second time in your document, you can then substitute the full citing for the short citation of "id". This "id" originates from the Latin word "idem", meaning the same, or repeated. The "id" short form should be used in the next use or reference to the citing/source if it's in the same section or refers to a single source. You can capitalize it to "Id" if it comes at the very beginning of a sentence. For example, once I make the full citation of *Strickland v. Washington,* 466 U.S. 668 (1984), I can then simply cite, *Strickland, id.*, when I refer to the same citing in the same section.

Where I refer to a legal citing in-between, I must then use the short citation of "supra" which means a citation was used previously or above. This is usually the case where you cite a source at the top of the page and then again at the bottom of the page, once you've asserted other citations or resources in between.

And so, the use of "id" after a citing or source means you are referring to that same source, having not used any others in between. And the use of "supra" means that you already cited the full source on the same page but used other sources or citations in-between.

I'll provide a short example for you as to the use of "supra" here:

"In *Strickland, supra*, the Supreme Court requires that the defendant first show that counsel's performance was deficient".

Well...do you see how it works? The use of short citations will save you a lot of time, will shorten the pages and will be better received by the reader(s).

Writing Tips

As I said initially, the whole purpose of writing legal documents is to communicate. Therefore, it's vital that your writing be accurate, clear and makes sense to the reader. You want your reader to receive the message that your writing is supposed to convey to them and that it's received in a professional light.

Proper spelling, grammar, and punctuation are vital parts of effective legal writing. Without them, your writing will not be well-received, and you will not win, simple as that.

In order to write well, you have to think well. If your mind is full of distractions, stress, or anxiety, it will show your inability to focus on the messages and issues you are trying to get across in your writing. Before you begin make certain you are not distracted, able to focus and concentrate fully on your writing.

What I tend to do is read case law followed by a *Black's Law Dictionary*, prior to any legal writing. This helps me to focus on the vocabulary, direction and message I want to relay to my readers. Then I associate myself with the arguments I intend to raise by going over the facts of the issues until I can recite them.

The truth is, first impressions really do leave the best impression, and this is nowhere truer than in the court. Therefore, you always want the first legal writing you send to immediately gain the respect of the reader, so that any additional writings or filings will receive the same respect/ attention of the reader. A document that fails to get the attention of the reader will also fail to get the hoped for and intended relief from the reader.

Simplification

In law school as well as in most paralegal schools, we are taught to write in a more linearly style, meaning from beginning, to middle, to end. However, as you can probably relate people simply don't read things in that order anymore, especially legal scholars, judges, etc.

People no longer take the long way in things and want everything to be as simple as possible. We need to have everything and to know everything up-front, at the very beginning...instead of at the end. We no longer have patience, or any sense of organization related to patience. It's now, now, now, we want it now.

Therefore, when you write, you should always lead with the conclusion. Do not bury the most important information where the reader may never see it if you have not persuaded him with your writing to continue reading. A judge, or any experienced legal reader today, will expect you to lead with your most important facts, points, or arguments and arrange them in descending order of importance. If you have not persuaded the reader by the second issue, it's very unlikely that you will in the fourth or fifth issue. If your best issue isn't enough then none of your issues will be, so list it up front.

United States Second Court of Appeals Judge Henry Friendly (deceased), once told a lawyer who said during oral arguments, "I've got five issues I'd like to argue before you today", "'Just give me your best one first."

That is exactly the way most judges and legal professionals think in society. Therefore, if you find yourself writing the words, "most important" in the middle of or at the end of your document, you've written a poor document, and it's likely your reader stopped reading long before.

If it's important, then put it first in your document. Your first shot is always better than those after, when your intended target is going away from you. Consider shooting a gun...the first shot at a deer, duck or whatever you are shooting at is most likely to hit its intended target, then those shots following when the object is further away.

And so, you need to "hit" the intended buttons of your reader while you have their immediate attention and interest. In today's world, nobody does anything on his own. We are all usually multitasking, especially if we are in society. Returning emails, updating a clerk, drinking coffee, checking text messages, etc., are all things that judges do while also reading your documents. And so, get to the point, and do so quickly.

The worst thing that most prison "writ writers" do is to go on, and on, and on, and on...for pages before quickly coming to a definitive conclusion at the end. Simply put...none of it was read, and you will not win. Think of a time you are riding in a car or walking to chow; we don't want to just sit there figuring out what to do. We just want to get to our destination as quickly as we possibly can and as easily.

Take a Break in Writing

Effective legal writing isn't easy, it takes time. It's irrational to think that you can sit down and write it all at once, especially if you are distracted with many other tasks, obligations, etc. When you write and find that you need to take a break or to finish the document at another time, I advise that you stop your writing while you are in the middle of a great argument, not when you finish it. I know it sounds crazy and counterproductive, but how many times have you stopped at a "good point" only to then struggle to begin again or to reorganize your thoughts? It happens to the best of us, even me. So, what I do...is what I just advised to you.

Instead of stopping at the end, I stop instead in the middle of a sentence or thought. That way, I'll have a great place to just jump right in and keep it all flowing. It's easier to finish a thought than it is to just think up another.

Checking Your Writing

In addition to spelling, grammar and punctuation, correct word choice is vital in all legal documents. Many words in English are routinely and often confused. If you use the incorrect word, you change the entire meaning of the document which often confuses the reader. Words such as: guilty and liable, oral and verbal, overrule and reverse and principal and principle are especially important for legal writers to understand. You should have a dictionary handy and look up words that you are unsure of. Watch for words that are commonly confused when you are editing and revising your work.

Make sure to check your writing for the following:

Redundancies

Legal writing should be clear and concise. Remove any repeated words or ideas.

Redundant: Because there aren't any other cases like this, we will research this unique cases' past history.

Better: Where this case is unique, we will research its history.

Sentence fragments

A sentence fragment fails to complete a thought.

Incorrect: Because the trial starts tomorrow.

Correct: The trial starts tomorrow.

Pronouns

Look for pronouns and make sure they agree with their antecedents.

Incorrect: Your firm represented my brother. They wanted me to contact you.

Correct: Your firm represented my brother. He wanted me to contact you.

Transition Words

These words add clarity to the writing and make it flow better.

Incorrect: Ice prevented the car from stopping in time. The city hadn't salted the road.

Correct: Ice prevented the car from stopping in time. Furthermore, the city hadn't salted the road.

Active Voice

Writing in an active voice, instead of a passive voice, gives your writing more forcefulness.

Passive: The defendant was found guilty by the jury.

Active: The jury found the defendant guilty.

Brevity/Wordiness

Legal documents should state a message in as few words as possible.

Wordy: I will mail my memorandum tomorrow due to the fact that today is a holiday.

Better: Today is a holiday so I will mail the memorandum tomorrow.

Using an active voice in your writing is one of the most important things you can ever do. Consider it like this: when you are active, you are then doing things. But, if you are passive, things are then being done *to* you. It's the same with subjects of sentences. In the active voice, the subject of your writing does something. (The jury found the defendant guilty.) In the passive voice, something is done to the subject/you. (The defendant was found guilty by the jury.)

The active voice has numerous advantages to you such as:

- It makes the writing more alive
- It uses fewer words
- It makes reading the writing easier
- It puts things in a chronological order

Single Word Translations

Prison "writ writers" are the worst at bloating their motions with the unnecessary use of words when a single word will suffice. This causes the reader to get lost in the wording, which takes away from what the writing is supposed to achieve. Let me give you some examples:

Bloated Writing:	*Single Word*:
On the ground that	Because
The majority of	Most
Subsequent to	After
Prior to	Before
Is able to	Can
At the present time	Now
During the course of	During
Submit an application	Apply
Conduct examination of	Examine

I think you understand what I am trying to say here, right? Keep it simple and keep it short. Otherwise you will only serve to alienate your reader, thus keeping you from obtaining the relief you are seeking.

Now, let's talk about the second biggest mistake that prisoners usually make in their legal writing, using *way* too much case law and argument.

Legal Argument and Case Law

I cringe at 99 percent of the legal writings I review of prisoners, or "writ writers". There is simply way too much use of case citations and too much argument. Even lawyers include too many case citations in their filings.

No matter how much research you do in the law library or in books, you don't need to include it all in your writings. In fact, that's the very worst thing you can do. Using "string cites", (when you list case law one after another), is fine, but you should never use more than three cases in any string. Never, have I heard a judge say, "These first five cases do nothing for me, but this sixth one...that's the winner!"

Case law doesn't win relief, the facts do. If you give judges one hundred "on point" case citations, they still won't always be able to make a fact-based decision. However, if you provide them with persuasive facts and no case law at all, they are still capable of making a decision. Why? Because they already know all of the case citings...they wrote them. What judges do not know are the facts of your particular case so that they can then apply the correct law to them. Get it? So, stop using so much case law, or don't start in the first place.

A brief or memorandum is not an examination or test. You don't have to prove to the judges that you know a lot of case law. Rather, they are to give them only the information needed to support the results you are then seeking from them. The truth is the more you analyze case law in your legal writing, the less you tend to give them good argument. You are focusing on the wrong thing and will never obtain the relief you are seeking.

When you do cite case law, you need to explain *why* you did so. This only needs to be done in a phrase, a clause or in parenthesis. When you do use case law, be sure to point out the details that distinguish your case from the precedent. Never ever, ever, ever, ever ask a court to overrule the case law that is working against you. Trial judges must follow the law of the jurisdiction and so must appellate panels not acting *en banc*. If you ask them to do so you will lose, period.

In some one-in-a-million cases, lawyers will decide that their best shot is to try to change an existing precedent. If that's your strategy especially as a pro se writer, be straightforward about it if you are hell-bent on doing so. Again, I tell you...Do not attempt it!

You should also be using case law from within your jurisdiction. Legal writing should always be localized. If you are arguing in a Texas court, the judges there don't care about the decisions of the Oklahoma courts. Judges who see you doing this will assume that you were unable to locate supporting case law in their own jurisdiction, which makes your argument appear weak.

As you list the case law from your local jurisdiction, do not cite them in the middle of your argument. This interrupts the flow. Of course, we have to use case law in our legal writing; it comes with the territory. But there are always ways to use them that make them far less disruptive, since even judges tend to skim over them. First move citings to the end of your sentences. That means to do so like this:

"In 1985, the United States Supreme Court held that defendants are entitled to the assistance of an expert witness." See *Ake v. Oklahoma*, 470 U.S. 68, 105 S. Ct. 1087, 84 L.ed.2d 53 (1985).

This keeps the reader from getting their train of thought lost with the interruption of case law (citations). What you are attempting to do is win relief based on the facts of your case supported by decisions of your jurisdiction. It's as simple as that.

Keep Your Emotions in Check

Effective legal writing should be a clash in ideas, not personalities. The more you attack and belittle your opponents (prosecutor) or comment on their ethical or moral inadequacies, the more you degrade yourself by doing so. It is therefore less likely you will win relief. Never mention your opponent in your writings.

Even comments like, "The appellee's reliance on these precedents are very misplaced," are an attempt to move the discussions away from your ideas and argument. It makes you appear childish, pretentious at best. You have no idea if the other side's reliance on those cases was misplaced or not. If you feel like you must challenge the other side's argument, just do so straight-out by saying something like, "The cases cited by the appellee do not apply in this matter," or something similar to one of my favorite writings by Jacob Stein and his associates, who wrote in the beginning of a Supreme Court brief in *Richardson-Merrell, Inc. v. Koller*, 472 U.S. 424 (1985) (footnotes omitted):

"From the record thus amassed the material facts emerged essentially undisputed. Petitioner's statement distorts that record, and thus we are compelled to set forth the facts in a comprehensive manner."

Never write one like this:

"With all due respect for my counterpart, I must tell this court that the appellee is lying and are in a conspiracy against me."

In fact, don't ever write either example. They are merely meant for an example. Remember to keep it short, simple and clean. Attack the position of your opponent, not the opponent personally.

Write As You Speak

In most pro se legal writing, there is evidence of stuffiness, whiny, defensive or psychotic tone. You should avoid sounding like any of these things. The best approach, of course, is to just relax and be normal. In talking as if you were talking to a friend or family member, you will in fact sound confident. Good legal writing, after all, is simply speech that has been polished and cleaned up. In general, if you wouldn't say it to your mother or your minister, then don't write it. Write your legal documents as you would speak to a judge in a courtroom.

Use proper English, drop the slang and the street talk. Also, don't try to sound like a judge or lawyer. It won't get you very far.

Notes:

Chapter Two: Persuasive Writing

There are five main goals in persuasive writing:

- Make it interesting
- Smooth transition
- Focus the argument
- Get your point across up-front
- Quote very smartly

Nearly all pro se "writ writers" fail to accomplish any of these goals, and it is reflected in their writings. Let's explore how you can attain all of these goals, shall we?

The Introduction

An ideal introduction should effectively state the issues in a way that can be understood by any reader upon their first reading. Completely absent of any extraneous matter, the introduction serves as the presentation of your ideas to the reader.

In nearly all jurisdictions, you are allowed to include a preliminary statement on the first page of your brief, memorandum, letter, etc. Even if the rules don't ask you to do so, go ahead and put it in there at the front. So, how do you choose what you should put into the introduction? That depends on how many arguments you are intending to make.

Let's say you only present a single issue. It might begin like this:

Motion for DNA Testing

Preliminary Statement

In determining this motion, the court faces the following issue:

Texas Code of Criminal Procedure. Ann. 64.01 et seq allows for the testing of forensic DNA evidence in a post-conviction challenge. Finding now that another person has confessed to the crime, is the appellant now entitled to state-funded DNA testing?

When you add an introduction, the judges will be grateful.

The Middle

In the middle of your legal writing, also known as the "heart" of the writing, is where you should develop the reasoning as to why you should win or lose your argument. How do you do that? First you need to choose the best ideas and case law that support your conclusion. Then you arrange them in a way that leads to your conclusions. All of the main headings and subheadings should drive the reader toward your ideas and conclusions.

Let's say that you have three issues to present to the court. You'll then have three parts in the body, typically from the strongest to the weakest. (Don't waste your time on the weak arguments.) Each part will have four intentions:

- Show the legal rule of your issue.
- Show how the facts in your issues meet that rule.
- Deal with your counterpart's arguments against you.
- Reinforce your points with additional reasons.

The Closing

This is where you sum up your arguments. If you want to better your chances at relief, you should answer the question posed in your introduction. Just as your introduction is important, so is your closing. It is your chance to sum up...preferably in a fresh and more expansive way, all of your arguments. The pro se "writ writers" that always begin with, "Wherefore, premises considered," have basically committed legal writing suicide. The same applies to closing with that statement. It says absolutely nothing to your reader.

For a forceful and effective closing reiterate your main points and argument as concisely as possible, and if you can, use fresh arguments. Don't say, "the foregoing reasons" or "the aforementioned argument", unless you have in fact first delivered a solid and authoritative introduction, middle, etc.

In reviewing a lot of pro se legal writings, as well as some written by attorneys, I'd say that around 85 percent of them have generic stock introductions and closings. They focus mostly the middle and not a very good middle at that. This defect of any logical structure, more than anything else, explains why so much of the pro-se prison "writ writer's" writings are inadequate at best.

The Judge's Perspective

In legal writing, there is an inevitable battle of roles. Brief writing isn't easy for anyone including skilled lawyers. That, however, doesn't apply to judges who read those briefs, memorandums or other legal writing. No matter how ground shaking and important your case seems to you, it is just one of thousands to them, just another day at the office. You need to refrain from the temptation to overhype the importance of your case and subject matter. If your case truly is significant and important, that will become apparent to the judges involved. If you do your research, you will discover that most of the brilliant and amazing legal writings, briefs, etc., written over the decades are ridiculously understated.

Also, consider how busy judges are, how many legal writings, motions, hearings and orders they deal with every day. For example, if you are then arguing for habeas corpus relief for ineffective assistance of counsel, the standards and arguments are virtually the same in every other case they see: likelihood of success on the merits, irreparable harm, balance of power and a weighing of the evidence as well as public interest. In effect, your case is the same to them as all of the others they deal with every single day. Always consider the judges when you are writing. When asking them to rule in your favor, the judges need to know what granting you relief will entail.

Control Your Ego

In quoting G. K. Chesterton, "A good legal writing tells us about the truth of the matter, but a bad legal writing tells us the truth about its writer." The arguments in your legal writings aren't about you personally, they are about the legal principles, procedures and precedent the courts should use in your case. The more you call attention to yourself as the writer by your use of big words, hostility, conspiracy theories, accusations and poor writing, the less effective you will be.

Your writings shouldn't attempt to be flashy, verbose or full of jargon. They should be conversational and understandable, without any exceptions. You are not legally trained, no matter how many days, years or months you have spent in the law library, and it will always show in your legal writing. So don't attempt to write like a lawyer; it will only serve to bring out the critical judgment of those who actually read your writings, such as judges (who are all lawyers) and their staff (who are usually also either former prosecutors or defense lawyers).

Those of us with legal training and education can quickly detect those who lack either. Additionally, it's far better to seem "inadequate" in your writings in order to entice the mercy of the court than to seem like you in fact know everything. If you promote yourself as if you can effectively act as a lawyer does, then you will be expected to walk-the-walk by the courts. It's not a very smart practice, so you're better off in not doing it.

Unless you or your conduct is at issue, refrain from saying things like, "I think", or "I feel". Also, it's hard enough to be funny when speaking; it's impossible to be humorous in legal writing. Recently I read a habeas corpus by an inmate "writ writer" who attempted humor. As was cited in the court's order, they didn't see the humor in it at all. It was likely the cause of his denial of relief. So, where humor is intended, don't even try it. My law professor once told me where I attempted humor in one of my assignments, "People don't buy from clowns". Ouch! (He gave me a C+.)

Try Using History

All readers generally enjoy history. Even more, where interpretations of the past can differ, most readers tend to treat historical narratives as facts. While legislative history can be deadly, although necessary, other historical explanations are anything but. Tell judges the circumstances that led to the passage of key statutes and penal codes that affect the law in your case.

Historical overviews can often be done in the fact section; it's not wise to do so in the argument section, adding to their persuasiveness and the appearance of objectivity. As Supreme Court Justice Holmes once said, "Sometimes a page of history is worth a volume of logic".

Now I'm not saying whether you should or shouldn't use history in your legal and persuasive writings. I'm simply saying that I have used history successfully in assisting other inmates, and perhaps you may be successful as well.

Trial Testimony

In just about every appellate brief I've read by a pro se legal writer, I have been taken on a chronological tour of the trial, relating witness by witness what the facts were and what happened, e.g., "The first witness said...then the second witness said...and at that point in the trial...."

Most of the time, this is not a good way to write your facts. Your sole job is to take the facts and make them into a story highlighting those you want readers to remember most, specifically what you want the judges to remember. While you are bound by both the laws and rules on appeal as well as the record, you cannot relitigate facts. You are not a stenographer whose job it is to relate what happened in the precise, order it happened. If, however, you are focusing on specific trial events, perhaps arguing the sufficiency of the evidence (which isn't allowed in a Texas 11.07 habeas) or the abuse of the judge's discretion for denying a motion (which also isn't cognizable in a Texas 11.07 habeas), then you should obviously take your readers through the relevant part of the trial, often word-for-word.

Questions Presented Section (In the Appeal Application)

The rules on how to present questions for arguments will vary from court to court. A few jurisdictions require the appellant to submit their version of the questions within weeks of appealing their cases. Others simply ask that the questions be included in the brief, such as Texas.

In either case, the same rules apply. Writing questions presented is a lot like writing argument headings. As with those headings, you want your questions to frame the issues in a way that makes your argument. It's tougher, however, for a reader to digest a long question rather than a long statement. Therefore, you should strive to make your questions twenty words of less. To make this easy, don't be afraid to divide your questions into sections, as in:

Were appellant's constitutional rights violated when:

- Trial counsel failed to investigate witnesses
- Trial counsel failed to call alibi witness
- Alibi witness was not called to testify

Of course, lengthier questions can be made to work occasionally, as this one did, filed by the Washington lawyer, Andrew L. Frey., in *Los Angeles Land Co. v. Brunswick Corp.*, 6 F.3d 1422 (9th Cir. 1993):

Whether the defendant can be labeled a "monopolist" under Section 2 of the Sherman Act because he owned the only bowling alley in a small town, even though uncontradicted evidence showed that defendant lacked power to exclude competition or control the prices.

Though the aforementioned was a civil litigation case (I practice both) it's a good example of dividing the question into separate parts to strengthen the content of it. This is especially wise and successful in criminal appeals, where all it takes for a reversal is one fundamental mistake. By highlighting three to four points within the context of a major one, you may make several more likely, and you will keep your argument focused. In both law school and paralegal advanced training, we are taught to do this, and it works.

Respect the Lower Courts

It's no secret, and contrary to what "writ writer's" want to believe, judges don't like to reverse their colleagues; they realize how much that hurts when it happens to them. Nothing in most of our prison lives, or outside professional careers, compares to the embarrassment and sting of a public rebuke or bashing from a higher court for lower court judges.

This realization should affect the legal writings of all pro se applicants. While you don't want to come across as depressing, you should raise your issues more in sorrow than in anger. When writing of judicial errors at trial, be direct and stick to the facts. U.S. Court of Appeals Judge John Wisdom told his clerks, "Do not say 'the district court failed' to consider, or anything like it. Treat district judges tenderly".

If you can do it well enough, take the lower court's language and use that to your own benefit. Pay extra attention to what I just wrote regarding the U.S. Court of Appeals Judge. He told his clerks how to write their opinions of the lower district court failures. What I've often told pro-se inmates is that it is very unlikely that a judge will ever see, let alone even read their writings. There are clerks in multiple levels of the courts who are lawyers. They screen every filing. It only progresses through the system, if...those clerks believe there is merit. Otherwise it will be denied; those clerks will write the opinion for the judges and simply have them sign it. Therefore, it's so important not to offend those clerk/lawyers...by acting as if you are a lawyer. They will not take that lightly.

Narrow vs. Broad Grounds

Simply stated the narrower your appeal is, the more likely it is that you will win agreement and not provoke a dissent and en banc reversal. Any phrases such as: "This case is not like..." and "This case will not require breaking new ground" can absolutely help you.

Appellate courts usually reverse on errors of law, thus a challenge to the sufficiency of the evidence will rarely, if ever, obtain relief. In Texas, as in many states, insufficiency of the evidence cannot be raised on habeas challenge for the first time. It must be argued on direct appeal only.

Judges who rule for criminal defendants know that they may be putting a law breaker back on the streets. This doesn't make them especially enthusiastic about granting you relief. You absolutely must address this issue head-on by stressing the broader value involved in upholding your constitutional rights. You should do this in a manner that treats law enforcement respectfully.

Reply Briefs

Many judges will tell you that filing reply briefs rarely make a difference. Where you are simply rearguing the same issues, you made in the initial filing, they rarely, if ever, even read it. It's never a good decision to file a reply brief if you have nothing new to offer.

On the other hand, Supreme Court Justice Anthony Scalia, in his book, said that he usually only read the reply brief because, "It was shorter". Can you remember what I said previously about the time constraints of judges? I rest my case on that issue. However, when and if you do decide to file a reply brief you want to keep it focused and short, rarely more than five pages no matter how numerous or complex the issues are. Anything longer absolutely will not be read, no exceptions.

In your first paragraph, you can review the principle points you made in your earlier filing, but it's not required. The key is to use the first or the following paragraphs to summarize the two or three primary arguments you want to answer in your reply. You should focus on major themes and new points, not on answering cases and rearguing old ones.

In short (in my opinion and training) replying to an opponent's reply brief such as the federal habeas is not only a waste of time, most courts won't allow it anyway. Unless the court requests it...just do not do it.

Cracking the Code of Persuasion (In Legal Writing)

In simple terms, legal writing requires its readers to make a split-second decision, based only on words. Whether a judge buys into your argument, for lack of a better word, depends on four factors: simplicity, self-interest, confidence, and empathy. These four factors are the same in the business sales industry, as well as in every scam related crime on earth. As taught in about every sales course related to door-to-door or telemarketing sales, this five-part mixture of influence (better known as SPICE) is a lethal tool.

Wondering what the fifth key component was in addition to simplicity, self-interest, confidence, and empathy? Well...it is called...incongruity. In full use this SPICE mixture of persuasion can get you whatever you want, without exception, either in person, over the phone or in writing: reservations, contracts, bargains, babies, appellate relief...anything. Used properly, it is a very useful process.

I, having taken this SPICE course in numerous different applications throughout my career, can attest to its power. In my most recent position, I applied this technique every single day, and accomplished what others in my field could not. Why? They didn't know how it worked or how to use it effectively even if they did know about it. In 2014, I set an industry record of five million dollars ($ 5,000,000) in unsolicited sales after first contact. My closing percentage was around ninety-five.

The understanding begins with a simple idea that some of us are better at the art of persuasion than others. And that with persuasion, just as with everything else, there exists a spectrum of talent along which each of us has our place. Judges are used to doing the persuading...not being persuaded.

I know...you would think the contrary was true, but it's not.

Example? Sure...

Judge: I find you guilty as charged and sentence you to pay a fine of $200 dollars. You can either pay in full within the allotted time of three weeks, or less if you pay today. Which shall it be?

Convict: Well, I only have $52 dollars on me right now, sir. But if you allow me a few minutes with the jury, I'd prefer to pay you now.

Guess what happens next. Yep...the judge lowers the fine! Success...

Even the Bible shows an example of the SPICE technique used by Jesus.

In the Gospel of St. John, for example, Jesus was essentially cornered by the Pharisees, who were presenting him with a woman accused of adultery and prostitution. They were seeking advice as to her punishment.

"Master", they say, "This woman was taken in adultery and prostitution. Moses instructs that such an act should be punished by stoning her to death. What do you say?" The truth is the Pharisees weren't really interested in Jesus's moral take on the matter. And Jesus knew it. Instead, their motives are less. What they were attempting to do is get Jesus involved in a legal argument. According to Mosaic law, the woman, as scribes correctly point out, should be stoned to death. But the Palestine that was now under Roman occupation had changed. Mosaic law had changed to Roman law and if Jesus upheld the former over the new, he would be open to the inevitable charge of inciting a riot. But that was the least of his worries. A crowd had gathered, and tensions were high according to Scripture. Getting out of this, it would seem, is a very hard task even for the smoothest of the smooth talkers let alone a mere carpenter with no rhetorical training whatsoever. What happened next is described like this:

> They said, tempting him that they might have to accuse him. But Jesus *stooped down*, and with his finger wrote on the ground, as though he hadn't heard them. So, when they continued asking him, he *lifted up himself*, and said unto them, "He that is without sin among you, let him first cast a stone at her". And again, he *stooped down*, and wrote on the ground. And they which heard it, being convicted by their own conscience, went out one by one, and Jesus was left alone, and the woman standing in the midst. John 8:3-9; author's emphasis)

This passage is unique. It's the only recorded occasion in the entire New Testament during which Jesus writes anything. Speculation is strong amongst biblical scholars, from what I have read, as to what those words might have been. But, that's not the issue of Jesus's actions in that situation.

Of course, it makes zero sense that he would feel the need to write anything at all. What I propose to you is that it wasn't the writing that Jesus was focused on, but merely the *action* of the writing. Using the SPICE technique taught to the elite sales force, let's look at Jesus's body language during his encounter with the Pharisees, aka, his "judgers".

The exchange, in fact, encompasses three distinct phases of SPICE. On first being challenged, what was his first initial reaction? Well, we note from the text that he immediately "stoops down" (antithesis, incongruity, appeasement). Then, when the elders persist in their sophistry, he "lifts himself" back up again to deliver his famous words (confidence, assertiveness) before reverting back to a stooping position and resuming his appeasement.

This was the classic sales technique of shifting and stealing momentum, what we also know in the business world as, "the take-away close". Here's how it works: When your customer or future client is being assertive and strong in their reasons for not doing business with you, for whatever reason, you make the quick transfer of power by standing up, reaching out your hand, and saying, "Now that I think about it, I'm not sure you'd be the right client or customer for me," and then sitting back down. In this technique, we use not just one language with our potential customer, but two languages: one modern, vocal and one ancient and powerful, silence.

And so, you are asking right now... "How does that apply to my legal writing?" The answer is relatively simple. Judges are expecting you to plead your innocence, how your trial was flawed, how you had a horse-shit attorney, etc. As well, they expect you to argue it all in the middle and end of your brief. When in fact you *don't* do what they expect, its re-programs their training and thought process. They are essentially thrown off task, and more susceptible to seeing things *your* way.

Place your argument in the beginning of your brief, as I told you earlier. And follow all the other instructions detailed in the previous chapters. Most of them are written with the SPICE methods in mind. They work. Research has repeatedly shown that top salesman and businessmen often lean slightly forward toward their clients when doing deals, a double whammy, signifying not only empathy (through increased proximity) but also a very sneaky subservience move. I used to use this method all the time with my kids.

The next time you find yourself having to lay down the law with a kid, try doing the opposite of what you normally would do. Rather than towering over them, draw them up close, crouch down to their level and then in as calm a tone as possible (I know...it is hard) say what you have to say. It also works in legal writing, emails, voice messages, texts and any other type of communication. Bringing yourself down to someone else's level in any way, shape or form, is a strong power move. What you are essentially saying (without saying it) is this,

"Look-it's not just you that's in the shit here. It's *both* of us. So why don't we see if we can't work out a deal?"

From the day we were born, we possessed the ability to persuade. It's all about marketing, and legal writing is no different. Baby chimps fuss, chicks squawk, etc. Consider the enormous challenges we faced at birth. From minute one, we had to influence those around us without thought, language, control of bodily functions, to take care of us. We had to persuade them. That ability never leaves us in that we have to persuade people to be our friends, spouses, to hire us, not give us a ticket, etc.

So, in our legal writings we must tap into that power of persuasion that we have always had and use every day, whether we know it or not. We have to put ourselves on the level of our readers, who are clerks, lawyers and of course judges. The first step is realizing, as I said previously, that we aren't as important to them as we believe we are. Instead, we are just another case number, not even a name. And so, in our legal writings, we must not come across as seeming "important", or "needy".

We must show respect for the judge's time constraints, by getting to the point of our issues as quickly as possible in our writings. We need to show them (1) what the issue is, (2) what the law is on the issue, (3) how that law was violated and (4) what we want them to do about it. In doing so, it persuades the judges that we just might be right.

This is true in all legal writings, letters, emails, text messages, etc. We always have a purpose in our writings, and how we express and obtain that purpose goes to the same SPICE characteristics inside of us all. Legal writing isn't always just about briefs or memorandums and motions. There are numerous other forms of legal applications in writing where persuasion is critical in whether we will get our desired results.

In the next chapter, we will talk about some of these different and usual types of legal writing. Where applicable, I will show you some techniques and rules related to those writings. Since we are all under the tick-tock of the clock...let's get to it.

Notes:

Chapter Three: Legal Letters

More of your time will be spent writing legal letters to clerks, lawyers and other legal professionals and organizations, rather than on any other appeal or legal purpose. You may need to request your client file, trial records, and open record requests, file motions, reply to motions, seek representation and possibly interact with innocence projects, etc.

And even though you might be in prison, you may still have a need for various legal letters to mortgage companies, banks, insurance companies, military agencies, schools, etc. Therefore, it's imperative that you understand how to write properly and effectively.

Though the format and structure of legal letters are not as strict as are other legal writings and filings, there are still some very important and vital things you must know. You must always draft your legal letters to best fit your situation, intent and purposes. No two are ever the same.

Let's get down to it, shall we?

Letterhead

Almost every prison writ writer tends to put letterhead on top of their legal letters. This is not required; moreover, it's improper unless you are part of a business or organization. It includes the business name, address, telephone number, etc., none of which, other than name and address applies to an inmate. Instead, at the conclusion of your legal letter, you should apply the name, prison number and address in the following manner:

Name

Inmate Number

Address

City, State and Zip

Of course, if you are not in prison and are with a business or using a letterhead of your own, you can provide that information at the top of the first page, in the center of the page. After the first page, the subsequent pages should have the header in the upper left corner of the paper.

Name
Page Two
October 31, 2019

Date

It's important for you to put the date on all your legal letters. It should include the month, day and year. You should always put the date that you will be *mailing* the letter and not the date you are writing it, unless they are the same day. You should place the date three lines below the letterhead, no matter if it's in the center of the page or the left side of the page. (Three lines means three pushes of the return button if you are typing). Of course, this only applies to the first page of the letter since the pages after that will look like the previous example (top left).

Mailing Notations

On occasion, you may want to mail your legal letter in a manner other than first class (regular mail). When doing so, you need to include the method in which you sent the letter, two lines below the date. It will look like this: (for inmates)

October 31, 2019

Via Certified Mail

Denton County District Attorney
[Address]

Inside Address

This part of the legal letter is mandatory since it won't arrive otherwise. This includes the addressee's name and address and is located two lines below the date or mailing notation on the left margin (left side) of the letter, as demonstrated above in the "Mailing Notations" section.

When writing the addressee's name, always be certain to include their title, as well, always spell their name and title correctly. Here's an example:

Mr. Richard Anderson, Esq.
Anderson Law Offices
100 Dover St
Dallas, TX 75201

Reference Line

Every legal letter should contain a reference line or subject line, so that the recipient knows what the letter is in reference to. Insert the reference line two lines below the inside address.

The reference line (abbreviated "Re:") should include the name of the case, the subject matter, the case number or file number, etc. See example below:

Re: State of Texas v. John Johnson

    Case No. F22-111-2222 Request for Trial Records

    Request for Trial Records

The reference line should always be in **bold** if typed.

Greeting

The greeting is the opening of your legal letter and should be located two lines below the reference line. Because legal letters are professional documents, the greeting you choose to open with should be professional. If you don't know the name of the person you are writing to, make every attempt to find out. Try to avoid beginning with a greeting like, "Dear Sir or Madam".

You will get a far better response when you humanize your recipient and call them by name (address them). If you are writing to a woman, use "Ms." unless you are absolutely certain that she is married or goes by a different title.

Dear Ms. Jackson:

Dear Mr. Jackson:

Body of Letter

When you begin the body of your letter, do so with an introduction or the purpose of the letter. This should begin two lines below your greeting. The introduction should only be one or two sentences and to the point.

The body of the letter follows the introduction and provides the rest of the information you need to communicate with the intended reader. When writing the body, be certain to target the right reader with your message. Also, make sure that you write in plain language and not in "legalese" or legal talk. Even if the topic you're covering is complex, your message should be as simple and clear as possible. The body gives the reader your intended message, so be specific and concise.

a. The **closing** of your letter will usually end with a basic statement indicating the end of the letter. Some common closing statements are:

- Thank you for your attention to this matter,
- Feel free to contact me with any further questions,
- I appreciate your assistance in this regard,

b. A **complimentary close** should be included two lines after your closing statement. The first letter of the complimentary close is always capitalized, and you should always follow the word or phrase with a comma. If you are addressing the letter to a judge, member of congress, a senator, etc., the complimentary closes with, "Sincerely", "Best regards", and "Very truly yours". The complimentary close is located two lines below the end of the body.

Signature

Four lines below the complimentary close, place your name (with title if you have one). If you're writing a letter to an attorney, however, you never add a title even if you have one. Your written signature goes between the complimentary close and the typed name. It looks like this:

Very respectfully,

Name, Inmate Number
Address
City, State and Zip

Copy and Notation/Enclosures

Occasionally, legal letters must be sent to more than one person. In those cases, use **copy notations** by writing "cc:" followed by the names of the other people to whom you mailed a copy of the letter. If you include other documents with the letter, you should include **enclosure notations** "Enc." for just one page or document, and "Encs". for multiple pages or documents.

This should be done in the lower left hand of the letter. See example below:

cc: Mr. Bruce Lee

Encs.

Organization and Formatting

Although legal letters don't all look the same or have specifically required formats, they should be professionally formatted in the ways I have listed up to this point. Legal letters are formatted this way because they are supposed to be business letters.

They can be full block, block or modified block styles.

- Full Block Style has all the information left justified, without paragraph indentations. (Like this book)

- Block Style has all the information at the left margin except for the date, the reference line, the complimentary close and the signature lines.

- Modified Block Style follows the same format as block style, except that the paragraphs are indented.

When formatting your legal letters, you should always:

- Use a common, readable typeface
- Write or print on letter sized paper (8 1/2 x 11); ·use single spaced paragraphs
- Choose a format and stick with it throughout the letter

There is nothing more important to a legal letter than organization. Before you write out or type (preferred method) your legal letter, you should first compose a draft consisting of your ideas, opinions and whatever research and information you have gathered.

As you begin your draft, follow the structure of your outline so that the letter flows in a comprehensible way. When you are organizing the letter, think about what information you should present first, second, third, etc. If you are including a sequence of events, be sure to put them in chronological order: beginning, middle and end.

Another way to organize your legal letter is to keep your ideas separate. If you are writing to your attorney regarding more than one issue, be sure to address each issue in its own paragraph.

Author Letter Writing Tips

Composing legal letters can be an intensive and thoughtful process; however, if you pay attention to the following rules you can create an effective legal letter:

- Write clearly and concisely (no legal jargon).
- Plan your letter in advance.
- Don't be wordy; keep it simple and short.
- Choose a format and stick with it.
- Always save a copy of your legal letter.
- Be certain that you included your intended documents.
- Edit and proofread your letter before mailing it.

Types of Legal Letters

There are many different types of legal letters that serve different purposes. Understanding the different types, styles and content of these letters will help you decide which one best suit your purpose and intent. Here a few different examples:

Confirming Letter

This is general correspondence that confirms some information. As an inmate, you will want to confirm any correspondence you ever receive from the courts, a clerk or your attorney. It looks like the following:

October 31, 2019

Mr. Jack Johnson, Attorney
100 Main St, Suite 200
Dallas, TX 75201

Re: State of Texas v. Brian Johnson
    Case No. F14-111-1111

    Extension of Time

Dear Mr. Johnson:

This letter is to confirm that you have filed for an extension of time to file my appellate brief. Can you please provide an estimated time frame for the brief to be then filed in the appellate court?

Respectfully,

Brian Johnson

Brian Johnson
Inmate Number
Address
City, State and Zip

Status Letters

This type of legal letter is used to obtain an update as to the progress of your case, appeal, status of requested documents or evidence, upcoming events or other important information. It may look like this:

October 31, 2019

Mr. Jack Johnson, Attorney
100 Main St., Suite 200
Dallas, TX 75201

Re: State of Texas v. Brian Johnson
    Case No. F14-111-1111

    Status Update

Dear Mr. Johnson:

At this time, I am writing to request a status update relative to my appeal. The last I was aware; you were awaiting the Reporter's Record from the Clerk.

I would appreciate any update you could provide at this time.

Respectfully,

Brian Johnson

Brian Johnson
Inmate Number
Address
City, State and Zip

Demand Letters

This type of letter tells the recipient that they need to take some action. You should express the exact actions you will take and what the consequences will be if they don't take immediate action. Be firm, but polite, and let the recipient know that there isn't any room for negotiations. You should always give a specific time frame or date in which you expect action, since "immediately" means different things to different people. Such a letter may look like this:

October 31, 2019

Mr. Jack Johnson
100 Main St, Suite 200
Dallas, TX 75201

Re: State of Texas v. Brian Johnson
    Case No. F14-111-1111
    Demand for Client File

Dear Mr. Johnson:

This is my second attempt to obtain my client file from your office. I need the client file in order to prepare for a post-conviction challenge to my conviction and sentence.

Unless you provide to me the full client file within ten (10) days receipt of this letter, I will file a Motion to Compel in the Court and refer you to the State Bar of Texas for disciplinary proceedings.

I appreciate your immediate attention to this matter.

Respectfully,

Brian Johnson

Brian Johnson
Inmate Number
Address
City, State and Zip

Chapter Four: Research Memorandums

Every single "writ writer" across the country in every prison, just said to themselves, "What is that?" That is because they don't write them and instead just jump right into writing the appellate memorandum. Commissary comes faster when the "job" is done, so to speak, which is their entire intent and purpose. Your relief or search of relief takes the backseat. That, in a lot of cases, ends your appellate abilities.

Effectively, you are "dead" by way of future appeals once the court denies your appeal for things like:

- Failing to state a claim
- Raising a non-meritorious claim
- Raising an already litigated claim
- Failing to state a ground for relief

There are three basic reasons why you should always write a research memorandum prior to writing your final appellate memorandum. First is to provide a clear and concise record of your legal research findings. Legal research is a multi-step process (not just reading books or case law) that involves investigation, analysis and writing.

Second is to compile the facts and analyze the chances of the court giving you the relief you seek or any relief at all. It's important to remain objective, so that you will know what and where to tweak the final memorandum.

Third is to answer the procedural questions you will encounter during your legal research. For instance, after you've done some research on what exactly constitutes possession of a controlled substance, you may want to know at that point if you also have a claim of failing to suppress the evidence.

Parts of a Legal Memorandum

Heading

This is the first part of the memorandum. The word "memorandum" is usually the first notation and should be capitalized and underlined. Of course, since this is simply the "investigative" findings structure and form are not required, though it is good practice since the final memorandum should follow your investigative version. If you're going to do it...do it right.

Facts (Issues)

This is where you will detail the significant facts you want to bring in your appellate memorandum. You should provide a balanced account of all the facts including any information that might show a weakness in your argument or issue.

Do not leave out any details, even if they work against you. This will help you fine-tune your arguments and choose which issues are most likely to get you relief. Try to keep everything in a chronological order.

Question(s) Presented (Rule)

After you have the facts or issues, you follow with the questions. This will help you to address the specific legal questions and theories from your research. Be as detailed as possible in this step.

Answers

This is where you answer the questions you posed. It should include a short statement that answers the question presented. Brief answers usually start with "Yes", "No", "Probably yes", or "No way". It's very important to be honest with yourself in this step, since lying to yourself will lead you to present weak issues to the appellate court thus denying you relief.

Analysis

This is the heart of your research memorandum. Here you will write what will effectively become your appellate memorandum. It's where you apply the law to your facts in order to see if you have a strong issue to present.

This is where you apply the IRAC method (as I have detailed) so that you can keep your analysis detailed, organized and effective.

Conclusion

Like the brief answer, the conclusion will include references to the significant facts of your case. Your conclusion should be guided by the precedent you were able to find in your research that supports your issues.

Explain the differences and similarities between the case law and the other resources and your case. Again, be honest, and don't try to fit the case law into your facts. This won't do you any good whatsoever.

I have included a sample Research Memorandum for your review:

RESEARCH MEMORANDUM

(For Brian Johnson)

Facts

On January 1, 2017 (New Year's Day), I was pulled over by a Dallas Police officer for failing to signal my blinker. My friend, John, was sitting in the passenger seat. When the officer approached my window, I rolled it down so that I could talk to him. At that point, the officer said that he smelled marijuana inside the car. He asked me to step outside of the car so he could search it. I told him that he could not search my car, but he said he had probable cause to search it. While searching the car, the officer found my wallet in the glove box. Inside, he discovered 3 grams of meth. The officer placed me under arrest, charging me with possession of a controlled substance.

My trial lawyer failed to file a motion to suppress the meth, challenging a reasonable expectation of privacy under the Fourth Amendment. I believe it was an illegal search, and that he didn't really smell marijuana since we hadn't smoked any marijuana.

Questions Presented

1. Did the officer have probable cause to search the car when he claimed to smell marijuana?

2. Did I have a reasonable expectation of privacy in my wallet, which was in glove compartment?

Answers to Questions Presented

Question #1:

Answer: Yes.

Probable cause by definition is, "A reasonable belief that a person has committed a crime". The test that the courts use to determine whether a probable cause exists for purposes of an arrest is whether facts and the circumstances within the officer's knowledge are sufficient to warrant a prudent person to believe a suspect has committed a crime or is about to commit a crime. Once that burden is met, an officer can search the vehicle for evidence of that crime.

Question #2:

Answer: Yes.

When a police officer makes a lawful arrest of the occupant of a car he may, as an incident to that arrest, search the passenger compartment of that car. However, an officer may not justify the investigation of a closed container or personal belonging located inside of the glove compartment or passenger compartment. My wallet lying inside the passenger compartment was not subject to an investigative search. It should not have been opened.

Analysis

I do not feel that the officer had a justified probable reason to search my car simply because he smelled marijuana. I did in fact fail to signal, which gave lawful reason to pull me over. The issue is whether or not the officer could search my car without proof that I had smoked marijuana.

The officer testified that I didn't signal, so he pulled me over. However, the Supreme Court has adopted a limited automobile exception under Article 1, § 9. So, the court will rule that the searching of my car was legal. But there is no known exception that allows officers to search my wallet that was in the glove box. In *White*, the Supreme Court said:

"Merely arresting someone does not give police carte blanche to search the personal property belonging to the arrestee without a warrant".

And so, my issue about my wallet is a good issue, but the issue about my car being searched is not. Also because of that Supreme Court ruling, my trial lawyer was ineffective for not filing a motion to suppress the meth.

Conclusion

I shouldn't challenge the searching of the car. I should challenge the search of my wallet as well as my trial lawyer's failure to suppress the drugs under the "fruits of the poisonous tree" doctrine.

- Due Process Violation (Fourth Amendment) for search of wallet
- Ineffective assistance of counsel (sixth amendment) for failing to file a motion to suppress the drugs found in my wallet.

Now, that you have written the practice memorandum...it's time to learn how to write the one that counts against you, or...for you. We call that the "Memorandum in Support".

Now shit gets interesting, so to speak.

Notes:

Chapter Five: Memorandums in Support

In the previous chapters we talked about persuasive writing and how it can help you to obtain relief in your case. Nowhere is that more important than in the Memorandum in Support of your appeal application/petition because that is meant to persuade the judge. In fact, that is its only purpose.

When writing a memorandum in support, keep in mind that it is incredibly important to be truthful, honest and transparent in what you write. The appellate courts have an exceptionally excellent grasp of the law and its interpretations. If you provide misleading information or misquote case law, they will quickly pick up on that which will destroy your appeal even if you have meritorious claims.

In order to persuade the courts to see your side, you must be subtle and agreeable in your persuasion techniques. Using a tone that rubs the judge the wrong way or leaving out case law that works against you in the standard will ruin your credibility in the eyes of the judge. Simply put, you will lose.

Let's show you how to write this monster.

Organization

As with the research memorandum, organization is very important here. Because your objective is to persuade the judge, you'll want to present your very strongest points first and then get back to them at the end of the section. By burying the potentially harmful facts in the middle of each section you will lead the reader, likely a judge at this point, to absorb the most helpful information first.

This way when the reader, whoever it may be, reaches the middle of the section they are subconsciously thinking about the information you've already given them. Yep, it's the old SPICE technique back in action. The reason behind this way of way of thinking is that emphasizing the information that's more favorable to you will make the reader think it's most important. You want the reader to believe that the harmful information doesn't carry as much weight and should therefore be a lesser factor when deciding your case.

Another technique that top sales professionals utilize in writing their bids or proposals is to present the positive information in short sentences, using an active voice. Negative information should be presented in longer sentences constructed in the passive voice. Why do you think that is? It makes your positive points appear to be basic, solid facts. The longer sentences presenting negative information will come off as you are being the victim of circumstance. Also, judges tend to read the shorter sentences due to their burdensome time constraints, meaning they will be getting mostly positive information.

Word Choice

This is critical because choosing the right words at the right time can convince the reader that your perspective is the correct one. Present your issues using strong, positive language. When presenting the opponent's position, use language that makes them sound weak, doubtful and far-fetched. You must do so in a polite and respectful manner.

For instance, as one of my favorite and often used in my writings:

"Lest this Court believe the stance of the appellee, I now provide precedent to the contrary that is far less cold".

What I effectively told the reader was that the case law being cited by the opposing party is not only wrong but old case law. As you can see, I did not use a lot of legal jargon, and I kept it short and to the point.

Contents of a Memorandum in Support

Most of the courts have their own guidelines in terms of how long a memorandum in support should be, what format you should use, etc. I've come to find that the following are what most courts require:

- Caption
- Preliminary Statement ·
- Questions Presented ·
- Statement of Facts ·
- Argument
- Conclusion

Additionally, if your memorandum is lengthy, you should include a table of contents and table of authorities. If for whatever reason, you feel that you need to exceed the requirements of your specific appellate court, you should request special permission from that court prior to writing the memo. A failure to do so will result in your memorandum being refused.

Caption

The caption of a memorandum in support presents the court with the basic information about the case. In most instances, it includes the following:

- Name of the court
- Name of the parties
- File number of the case
- Title of the memorandum

Preliminary Statement

This is also called the "introductory statement" because it tells the reader why the memorandum is being filed. It describes the events of the case that relate to the issues being addressed.

Questions Presented

This section of the memorandum discusses the questions that the appellant (you) want(s) the reader to think about and rule on. Again, at this stage, the reader will usually be a judge or magistrate. You should write this in an easy-to-understand, persuasive language and it should be informative and factual. Each question should focus on a single specific issue.

Statement of Facts

In some states, this is called the "statement of the case", since it provides an opportunity for you to tell the judge the facts that you want them to see. When writing this, the presentation of the facts should always favor you so that you persuade the judge to agree with your interpretation of the law.

However, this is not where you argue your case. You are only making a short statement related to the facts. Keep it clear, concise, and powerful. And keep it short.

Argument

This is the section that makes grown-ass men cry, where the work is done. This is also known as the "summary of argument" in some states, where you present a short summary of the points that will be argued in this section of the memorandum. Be sure to present the principle points in your case and what you intend to argue. This section takes a lot of practice to be effective. Paid attorneys fail in this section...so it is understandable if pro-se appellants do also.

Conclusion

If the legal issue is relatively basic, you might be able to conclude your memorandum in a single sentence. If the issues are more complex, or if you've named multiple issues, it's best to address every issue completely. Use persuasive language, strong, confident and precise.

Now...let me do what I do best...write freely. Let me prepare a fictional case to show you how to write a memorandum in support. Again, it's completely fictional and only intended to give you a written example.

Show time...

Raymond E. Lumsden

NO. 03-19-01234-CR

IN THE THIRD DISTRICT COURT OF APPEALS
DALLAS, TEXAS

JOHN DOE,

Appellant,

v.

THE STATE OF TEXAS

Appellee

MEMORANDUM IN SUPPORT

John Doe, Pro-Se
Inmate Number
Address
City, State and Zip

Preliminary Statement

Appellant John Doe submits this memorandum in support of an application for writ of habeas corpus in proving that his trial counsel provided him with ineffective assistance of counsel for failing to suppress evidence prior to trial, where police entered his home and seized without a warrant, without probable cause and without appellant's consent, evidence.

QUESTIONS PRESENTED

1. Did the law enforcement officers violate John Doe's constitutional rights against unreasonable search and seizure when the law enforcement officers coerced Doe under duress into opening a safe located in his home when the reason that the officers were at the residence was to aid Doe in response to a call that an intruder was in the process of forcefully then entering Doe's home?

2. Did Doe's trial attorney fail to file a motion to suppress the seized evidence prior to trial in violation of Doe's constitutional rights?

STATEMENTS OF FACTS

On January 1, 2015 appellant John Doe, a Dallas resident, called police to report that an unknown person was attempting to forcefully enter his residence. Doe also told the 911 operator that he had several guns locked in a safe inside of his bedroom closet. When responding to the call, Officer Anderson was met in the front yard by Doe.

Doe reported to Officer Anderson that an armed man had forced his way into the home. Officer Anderson then followed Doe into the home, where they did not find any intruder or signs of forced entry. Officer Anderson did, however, see the safe that Doe had mentioned. When Officer Anderson asked Doe to open the safe, Doe refused. Officer Anderson then warned Doe that if he didn't open it, they would place him under arrest, take him to jail and prosecute him.

Doe then opened the safe, and the officer discovered a plastic bag that contained a white powder as well as a large amount of U.S. currency. A measurement of the evidence later proved it to be 100 grams of cocaine and $50,000 in U.S. currency. At that point, Officer Anderson placed Doe under arrest.

SUMMARY OF THE ARGUMENT

The Appellant contends that the arresting officer acting under the color of law as agents of the government exceeded the scope of their authority by executing an illegal search and seizure upon the appellant's property.

Any consent the appellant gave to the opening of the safe was involuntary, and the contents of the safe confiscated as evidence must be suppressed. Any contraband found discovered after an illegal search must be suppressed.

LEGAL ARGUMENT

A. BECAUSE THE APPELLANT'S CONSENT TO THE SEARCH OF HIS SAFE WAS INVOLUNTARY, THE EVIDENCE FOUND INSIDE SHOULD BE SUPPRESSED AS THE FRUIT OF AN UNCONSTITUTIONAL SEARCH AND SEIZURE.

Under both the Fourth Amendment of the United States Constitution and Texas Constitution Art. 1, § 7, a search conducted without a warrant is deemed to be per se unreasonable. On motion, the court shall suppress evidence obtained by the state as a result of a search or seizure on the grounds that the search without a warrant was unreasonable and unlawful. Texas Penal Code 55 and Texas Rules of Criminal Procedure 77.1 The Fourth Amendment to the United States Constitution prohibits unreasonable searches and seizures. *See Walter v. United States*, 447 U.S. 649 (1995).

A warrantless search is presumptively unreasonable, so that the burden of proving justification for a warrantless arrest/search or seizure falls on the prosecution. *Id.* at 24. Because the search of the safe was conducted without a warrant, the State of Texas has the burden of then establishing justification under a recognized exception to the warrant requirement. See, *Smith v. State*, 123 F.3d 345 (2015).

In this case, the appellant opened the safe only because the officer threatened to arrest and prosecute him. Because of those threats without cause, they abused their authority. Therefore, because the search of the safe was unlawful, all evidence obtained from exploiting it must then be suppressed *Wong v. United States*, 371 U.S. 471, 487 (1963).

B. BECAUSE HIS TRIAL COUNSEL FAILED TO SUPPRESS THE EVIDENCE FROM THE SAFE, OBTAINED ILLEGALLY, APPELLANT RECEIVED INEFFECTIVE ASSISTANCE OF COUNSEL GUARANTEED UNDER THE SIXTH AMENDMENT.

Under the Sixth Amendment of the United States Constitution and the Texas Constitution, Art. 1, §10, defendants have the right to the effective assistance of counsel. The assessment as to whether a defendant received effective assistance of counsel must be made according to the facts of each case. *Ex parte Scott*, 581 S.W.2d 181 (Tex. Crim. App. 1979). To then prevail, the appellant must show: (1) counsel's performance was deficient to the extent that counsel failed to function as the counsel guaranteed by the Sixth Amendment; (2) there is a reasonable probability that, but for counsel's errors, the result of the proceeding would have been different. *Strickland v. Washington*, 466 U.S.

668, 104 S. Ct. 2052, 80 L.Ed. 2d 674 (1984); *Cox v. State*, 389 S.W.3d 817 (Tex. Crim. App. 2012).

In order to demonstrate that counsel rendered ineffective assistance of counsel for failing to file a motion to suppress, the defendant must show that the motion would have been successful. *Jackson v. State*, 973 S.W.2d 954 (Tex. Crim. App. 1998).

In the instant case, it is without question that Officer Anderson did not have a valid search warrant and had responded to the appellant's home-based call to 911 for assistance. Only when seeing the safe in the closet, did he then threaten to arrest and charge appellant if he didn't open the safe immediately. At no time did he attempt to obtain a warrant or even call for his supervisor to come to the home, as is procedure for an officer under Dallas Police rules and regulations. Instead, Officer Anderson chose to violate the constitutional rights assured to appellant under the United States Constitution's Fourth Amendment.

Then knowing this prior to trial, appellant's trial counsel had an ethical and professional duty to the appellant to fully investigate the facts surrounding his arrest, prepare an adversarial challenge to those arrest-related facts and challenge the illegal search and seizure by the filing of a motion to suppress the evidence discovered in that search.

CONCLUSION

Appellant John Doe consented to the search of his safe only because he was threatened with arrest and prosecution, where Officer Anderson without probable cause or warrant, told him essentially that he had no other choice. Only after opening the safe did Officer Anderson arrest appellant.

Because the search of the safe was done in an unconstitutional manner in this case, any and all evidence found in the safe was part of the "fruit of the poisonous tree," and this Court should reverse the conviction and remand for further proceedings.

Dated: November 1, 2019

John Doe, Pro Se

45

Related to the sample I just provided, keep in mind that it should be typed or written using double-spacing (I did not do so in attempt to save space). As for the case law and precedent most of it was actual except for the parts I could not access correct precedent, due to currently being on lockdown facility wide and unable to visit the law library. All the federal citation used was correct and true based solely on memory.

Where pro se inmates make the biggest mistake is over arguing their issues and making the memorandum too long, which lessens the probability that any judge will even read it. Keep it short, direct, strong and clear. If you are filing in the federal courts, you should review Rule 28 (Briefs) of the Federal Rules of Appellate Procedure. My book, *The Habeas Corpus Manual*, has those rules in detail as well as legal forms and motions that might be of great use to you.

I have decided not to include an example of an appellate brief, since most states now allow a memorandum in support to be filed along with their application for habeas relief, etc., essentially, the same thing as a brief. Additionally, those require far more detail, structure, form and length. It would only serve to confuse you in doing so. My suggestion is to attend the law library in your prison and read examples in the "holdings" section of the library catalogue. More so, I cannot express enough the importance of hiring an appeal attorney if you are able to do so. No matter how great of a "writ writer" you believe yourself to be...only a fool has himself as a client, and you will fail miserably in most cases.

That being said, there have been numerous successes by pro se appellants over the past five (5) years in many states. And so, where you cannot afford to hire counsel, there is hope if you follow the rules and write effectively.

Of course, you cannot write effectively unless you first understand the rules and precedents that the courts use determining cases on appeal. And so, let's teach you the proper way to do legal research, shall we?

Notes:

Chapter Six: The United States Legal System

Learning to conduct legal research efficiently and properly is essential to the smooth operation of the legal system, as well as to obtaining relief in your case. This isn't always easy and will require some hard work. Let's start from the very beginning since most of you have very little, if any, understanding of the legal system in general. Here we go...

Criminal v. Civil Law

In criminal law, the plaintiff is always the state or federal government. The plaintiff sues the defendant (through criminal charges) because he or she has allegedly violated a state or federal statute. Jury decisions in a criminal case must be unanimous, and the plaintiff must prove the defendant's guilt "beyond a reasonable doubt". Punishments may include fines, being put into prison, community service and in some cases (like Texas) the death penalty. A crime in a criminal case is classified into one of two broad categories: (1) a felony, which has a maximum sentence of more than one year of incarceration and (2) a misdemeanor, which has a maximum sentence of less than one year of incarceration.

In civil law the case is between individuals, a plaintiff and a defendant, in which the plaintiff sues for damages or other wrongs allegedly caused by a defendant. In a civil case it's the plaintiff's duty to prove the *prima facie* (at first glance) of his or her case by the preponderance of the evidence. This means the plaintiff must prove that the wrongdoing "more than likely" occurred. Civil cases involve only the payment of money for wrongdoings and not incarceration. If the defendant in a civil case loses, he or she reimburses the plaintiff for losses caused by his or her actions and behavior.

Procedural Law v. Substantive Law

Procedural law is the body of rules that governs how our rights are stated or determined for both individuals and groups. In other words, procedural law is used to create substantive law.

Substantive law refers to the body of rules that determines the individual and group rights. It includes all categories of law, including real estate, torts and criminal law.

Federal v. State Law

Federal law refers to the collective body of law that includes federal statutes found in the United States Code (U.S.C.), and the U.S. Constitution, rules, regulations, as well as decisions of federal administration agencies. This will also include the decisions of the federal court system.

Federal laws are specified in the in the U.S. Constitution and typically involve issues that affect the entire country, rather than the conduct of one person or persons in a particular place. Federal laws regulate foreign affairs, the military, aviation, railroads and trademarks. Since the U.S. Constitution was written over 200 years ago, it has been amended or changed in an attempt to "better" the laws.

State law on the other hand, refers to the collective body of law that includes state constitutions, state statutes, state administration agencies, state court decisions and local municipality laws and ordinances.

Steps in a Criminal Procedure

1. Arrest: An individual is either arrested or summoned by complaint.

Officers may also arrest without an official warrant if there is probable cause. An accused must be informed of their right to representation and against self-incrimination (Miranda Warning).

2. Bail: A deposit of money that helps to guarantee that an accused person will appear for trial as specified. This happens after the person has been taken into custody by law enforcement. If that person does not appear at the specified time, the bail may be forfeited, and the person considered a fugitive from justice.

3. Preliminary Hearing: A hearing that is held to determine whether there is probable cause for holding the accused for trial.

4. Arraignment: An arraignment hearing has three purposes: (1) to make identification; (2) to inform the accused of the charges; and (3) to obtain the plea of the accused: guilty, not guilty, or no contest.

5. Trial: The U.S. Constitution guarantees a right to a jury trial in a criminal matter; this right, however, may be waived by the defendant. A trial consists of 12 jurors, who are citizens, to listen to the facts and make their decision as to guilt.

Steps in a Civil Procedure

1. Complaint: The complaint states the specific injury suffered by the plaintiff, the acts the defendant(s) alleged to have caused that injury and the remedy, such as damages being sought.

2. Summons: This is the notice that the plaintiff must provide to the defendant informing them that a complaint has been filed, and that a response is due to be made. Once notice is received, the defendant must make some response to the summons and complaint within a specified time in order to avoid a default judgment.

3. Answer: This is where the defendant of the lawsuit responds to the factual allegations in the complaint. The answer must state any affirmative defenses that the defendant intends to use against the plaintiff's claims, or the defendant cannot then make them during trial. At this point, the defendant can file a crossclaim against the plaintiff and counter claims.

4. Discovery: This is where both sides will attempt to locate all the witnesses and uncover all evidence while learning as much as they can about the issues of the lawsuit.

5. Interrogatories: A written set of questions (normally 25) that you want the defendant to answer. The defendants may also require that you answer their questions in return.

6. Subpoena Issuance: This is where both sides will request the court to issue subpoenas for their witnesses to give testimony in court.

7. Pretrial Conference: This step is where both sides meet with the judge prior to trial to discuss the issues involved in the lawsuit. These conferences are not required in most states, however. Stipulations and agreements are often made between the parties at this stage.

8. Trial: When not agreed to prior to trial by settlement, the matters will be presented to either a jury or before a judge to determine the winner of the lawsuit.

Structure of the Federal Government

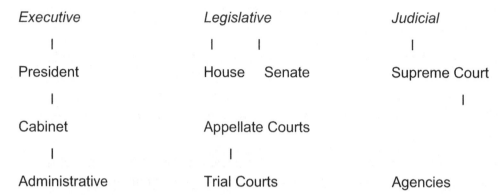

Executive	Legislative	Judicial
|	| |	|
President	House Senate	Supreme Court
|		|
Cabinet	Appellate Courts	
|	|	
Administrative	Trial Courts	Agencies

Structure of the State Government

Executive	Legislative	Judicial
|	| |	|
Governor	House Senate	High Court
|		|
Administrative	Appellate Court	Agencies
|		
Trial Court		

Appellate Court Circuits

First Circuit: Maine, Massachusetts, New Hampshire Puerto Rico and Rhode Island

Second Circuit: Connecticut, New York and Vermont

Third Circuit: Delaware, New Jersey, Pennsylvania and the Virgin Islands

Fourth Circuit: Maryland, North Carolina, South Carolina, Virginia and West Virginia

Fifth Circuit: Louisiana, Mississippi and Texas

Sixth Circuit: Kentucky, Michigan, Ohio and Tennessee

Seventh Circuit: Illinois, Indiana and Wisconsin

Eighth Circuit: Arkansas, Iowa, Minnesota, Missouri, Nebraska, North Dakota and South Dakota

Ninth Circuit: Alaska, Arizona, California, Guam, Hawaii, Idaho, Montana, Nevada, the Northern Mariana Islands, Oregon and Washington

Tenth Circuit: Colorado, Kansas, New Mexico, Oklahoma, Utah and Wyoming

Eleventh Circuit: Alabama, Florida and Georgia

Federal Circuit: United States

U.S. Supreme Court

The U.S. Supreme Court was established by the U.S. Constitution and is the highest court in the nation. One chief justice and eight associate justices serve on the Court. Justices are appointed by the President and confirmed by the Senate. The Supreme Court usually reviews less than 100 cases per year of more than 10,000 requests for review.

Court and Law Enforcement Personnel

Officers of the Court

The officers of the court are persons assembled at the court to administer justice. They include the judge who is the principle officer of the court, the lawyers, the clerk of the court, the sheriff, the marshal, the bailiff and possibly a constable or court officer.

Judges

A judge may be elected or appointed. From the time the oath of office is taken, judges at all levels are bound to conduct themselves in an ethical manner and to adhere to a code of judicial conduct. There are four canons in which a judge should conduct themselves:

- Canon 1: A judge shall uphold and promote the independence, integrity, and impartiality of the judiciary and shall avoid impropriety and the appearance of impropriety.

- Canon 2: A judge shall perform the duties of judicial office impartially, competently and diligently.

- Canon 3: A judge shall conduct the judge's personal and extrajudicial activities to minimize the risk of conflict with the obligation of judicial office.

- Canon 4 A judge or candidate for judicial office shall engage not in political or campaign activity that is inconsistent with the independence, integrity or impartiality of the judiciary

Chapter Seven: Law Library: Primary Sources

When you visit a law library you will find both primary and secondary sources of information. Primary sources are those that contain the law, such as: constitutions, statutes, and cases (common law). Secondary sources, on the other hand, contain writings about the law and not the law itself. These will be law journals, law reviews and legal encyclopedias. If you aren't sure where to find either of these sources, you can review the finding tools which will direct you to where to find primary and secondary sources.

Primary Sources:	*Secondary Sources:*
Constitutions	Legal Dictionaries
Case Law	Legal Encyclopedias
Statutes	Law Reviews & Periodicals
Administrative Rules	Treatises
Executive orders	American Law Reports
	Restatements
	Uniform Law & Model Acts

Codification

Once a law is passed, it is printed on parchment paper and signed by the President if it is federal law. If it's a state law, the governor signs it. A copy of that law must be made however, so it can be stored in law libraries and accessed by the public without cost. This duplication process is called a "slip law". Federal slip laws are published in the U.S. Code, which is a series of fifty (50) titles each covering different subject areas.

When a new law is passed, the relevant sections of the code are updated. For example, if a new statute is passed about crime and criminal procedure, then Title 18 would be modified.

Three publishers publish the U.S. Code. The first is the U.S. Government, and that is called the U.S.C. Two others publish annotated versions of the code, which is basically a one or-two-line summary of each statute referring the reader to cases relating to its interpretation. These publishers are the United

States Code Annotated (U.S.C.A.) and the United States Code Service (U.S.C.S.)

U.S.C.A. is published by West and is available on Westlaw, while U.S.C.S. is published by the Lawyers Cooperative Publishing Co. and is available on LexisNexis.

Where the U.S. Code cites statutes word for word, it is known as the official code. Since the U.S.C.A. and the U.S.C.S. only interpret the statute, they are considered the unofficial sources of code.

Court Cases

Courts and judges rule primarily on real-life controversies and write their opinions explaining their judgments. These opinions are called case law. When you are in a law library, you need to know which court this is, because case reporters (book of cases) are different for each (trial court/appellate court). For instance, on the federal level some trial court opinions are reported in the *Federal Supplement*. A greater percentage of appellate cases are published in the *Federal Reporter*. All U.S. Supreme Court cases are reported in three reporter sets, one official version and two produced by private publishers. (I was unable to uncover additional publishers)

Rulings in judicial cases are called precedents, meaning that later cases in certain courts must follow those rulings. That being said, cases may arise that have different facts and the ruling may be different. Also, the precedent may be from a court that does not have "binding authority" on the court deciding the new case. In this case the precedent may only have a "persuasive authority", meaning the new court may consider the precedent but is not bound by it. When doing your case law research, you need to be searching for cases like your case that are newer, so that you can argue that the older cases have different facts than your case.

Right now, you are thinking, "Should I use the U.S.C., THE U.S.C.A., or the U.S.C.S.?" And that's a good question to be asking. Let me explain...it all depends on what information you need to obtain. When deciding, keep this in mind:

- Use U.S.C. when you need the exact wording of a statute or when you need references to other resources such as cases that interpret statutes.

- U.S.C.A. and U.S.C.S. are essentially the same thing so you'll use one or the other. They provide resources to other sources in the library.

Chapter Eight: Law Library – Secondary Sources

For most pro-se researchers, secondary sources are where you want to start. They will lead you to primary resources more related to or, "on point" with your own case.

Secondary sources or "secondary authorities" are easier to read than most primary sources. They contain summarized information about legal documents and cases, which cuts down on the amount of text (writing) you have to go through. Because they are written by judges, lawyers, law professors and other legal commentators, many secondary sources not only explain details of a case but also offer case analyses as well.

Secondary sources are also helpful when you're searching a new or undeveloped area of the law, or when you're trying to gain a better understanding of a large or expansive area of law. You must remember that they cannot stand on their own because they aren't binding in courts. You cannot cite them in your briefs or memorandums. That requires primary sources. Let's quickly look at a couple of secondary sources.

Legal Periodicals

These are trade publications (written for a specific audience) for legal professionals including paralegals, lawyers, judges, etc. While many exist, there are a few that may assist you more than others:

1. Law Journals:

These contain articles offering commentaries and opinions on legislation, court decisions and other legal issues. Most articles focus on a specific area of law. The citations and footnotes will be helpful in directing you to additional information related to your topic/issue.

2: Legal Newspaper:

A legal newspaper publishes legal notices, court calendars and court cases. A few of these are, *The Recorder*, *The Legal Intelligencer*, etc. There is one legal periodical that I receive, called, *Criminal Law Bulletin*, published by Thomson Reuters.

Treatises

A treatise is a book that focuses on one specific area of law. It contains expansive information on a topic that receives only general treatment in a legal encyclopedia. Treatises are written by legal scholars and often will contain critical opinions about the law or court system.

Some treatises contain multiple volumes, such as *Section 1983 Litigation*, which is published by Aspen. Treatises can help you to support your research. Again, pay special attention to the footnotes at the bottom of the pages as they will often lead you to another source. While treatises are not binding on the courts, they are often very well respected by most appellate courts. You cannot cite them in your legal filings as binding; however, they are used as persuasive authority.

American Law Reports (ALR)

These are special periodicals that combine summaries of all court cases on an issue from every jurisdiction with essays (briefs/annotations) offering objective explanations. ALRs are especially important and provide a vast combination of both primary and secondary sources.

Restatements

These are books that are designed to help legal professionals understand the law by putting it into different language and offering explanations. In simple terms, they break down the law so it's easier to understand. There is usually an index to help you narrow down your search.

Because restatements are written by the American Law Institute (ALI), they are highly respected by judges and are often cited even though they aren't primary sources.

Chapter Nine: Computer-Assisted Legal Research (CALR)

"But I don't have access to a computer," the state prisoners are saying. I understand that, however, many states now offer CALR on tablets and on law library computers. Also, federal prisoners have computer access.

And so...let us get to it.

CALR v. Manual Research

The difference should be obvious, right? Well...there's more to it than that. When you conduct legal research with a computer, you are accessing thousands of databases. And though it's faster and easier, CALR should not replace doing manual research. Both are very important in combination.

When should you use one and not the other? Let's take a look:

CALR

- When you need to save time·
- You are searching unique terms ·
- You're searching a unique fact
- You need information that isn't published in print
- Your search is very narrow

Manual Research

- When you need general knowledge
- There is too much information on CALR
- You need access to very old case law
- You have complex issues
- Over common terms or issues

LexisNexis

Since this is the preferred CALR program by most prisons due to its pretty cheap pricing, I will start with it. Inmates usually know it by simply, Lexis.

Lexis provides the following legal resources:

- U.S. case law, including case summaries, Shepard's Citations and headnotes for all federal and state courts.
- U.S. statutes
- Law reviews and journals
- Canadian and European case law

Basic Commands

Command	Meaning
.ns	New search
.cf	Change file
.cm	Change menu
.cl	Change library
rel	Show related terms
thes	Thesaurus
.fd	Display first document
.np	Next page
.npn	Skip n pages forward
	(n + number of pages)
.nd	Next document
.rank	Rank documents by relevance
.sav	Save the search
.pr	Print the document

Terms and Connectors

Lexis allows you to use terms and connectors to find in-depth information about a subject. Terms are search words...connectors are characters that establish a logical relationship between terms. Lexis doesn't search for connectors in actual documents but instead searches for words they might represent.

Lexis allows you to enter more than one term and connector in a search. When you do this, Lexis prioritizes the terms and connectors like this:

1. OR
2. W/n
3. W/s
4. W/p
5. AND
6. AND/NOT

Lexis Connector:	Meaning:
Or	Links synonyms or alternate expressions such as acronyms, i.e., attorney or lawyer" will bring up documents with either "attorney" or "lawyer" in them.
W/n	Links words of phrases; the n stands for a number from 1-255; i.e., "restaurants W/3 violations" will find documents with the word "restaurant" within three or fewer words of "violation" regardless of which was first.
PRE/n	Finds both words in a document when the first word precedes the second word by n or fewer words. The letter stands for a number from 1-255; i.e. "U.S. PRE/2 air online" will find documents including the words "U.S. Air" or "U.S. Airlines".
NOT w/n	Requires the first word to be in the document; the second word may also appear, but it cannot be within n words of the first word.
W/s	Searches for documents with the search words in the same exact sentence.
W/p	Looks for documents with search words in the same paragraph.
AND	Searches documents with the words or phrases together anywhere in the document.
AND NOT	Does not retrieve documents that contain certain words or phrases.

[Provided in the NexisLexis User's Manual 2018]

Truncating

Lexis also allows you to use an exclamation point (!) to replace multiple letters at the end of a word. For example, you can type in *automo*! to get documents that contain the words automobile and automotive in the terms and connectors search mode (not natural language section). You can also use the asterisk (*) to replace a letter in a search. For example, you could type m*n to retrieve documents with the words man, and men in them.

Natural Language Search

In my opinion, having used Lexis for more than a decade, this is its best feature. Here you can simply ask Lexis a question like, "Can a grocery store be liable if a customer slips and falls on water, even if they didn't see or know about the water?"

While this will provide a lot of information it isn't very refined, and it isn't as limited as when you use terms and connectors.

How to Use Lexis

Option 1: Quick Search:

If you click on the Quick Search link, you'll see three options above the Enter Search Term Box: (1) Terms and Connectors, (2) Natural Language, (3) Easy Search. To choose which you want to use, click on the box.

Next, choose a jurisdiction from the drop-down menu. Then choose the practice from another drop-down menu (Employment, Labor, Liability, Criminal, Civil, Real Estate, etc.). If you want case law, you need to click on that box located in front of the jurisdictions.

Option 2: Find a Source:

Go back to the main screen where you can locate particular sources.

Under the search tab is an ALL tab. Click on the ALL tab, and you will find three headings:
(1) Legal, (2) News & Business and (3) Public Records.

If you click the Legal tab, you'll see what's called the Source Selection Hierarchy. There are many categories here that will benefit you.

Chapter Ten: Manual Legal Research

Let's start from the beginning...you first need to familiarize yourself with your prison law library. Doing this will save you a lot of frustration and time, because you will need to use it quite often in the appellate process, etc.

Unfortunately for you all law libraries are different and have resources others do not, and vice versa. However, all will have a "Holdings" list that tells you what resources they have available for you. In prison this is usually available by requesting it from the officer on duty there.

Conducting legal research is a time-consuming pain in the ass, and the law libraries in prisons are often very intimidating at first. Finding what you are looking for is rarely easy, so you need to be patient and maintain a positive attitude. Be aware that legal resources will sometimes contradict each other; that's part of the injustice of the system. Just when you think you have found a case supporting your issue, you'll find another that works against you. Breathe in... breathe out...and stay positive.

So, what questions do we need to answer before you begin your research?

- Is it criminal or civil?
- Is it a federal case, or a state case?
- Is it Procedural or Substantive?
- Jurisdiction?

Once these questions are answered, we turn to the books.

The Books

Most law books have very specific indexes which you'll use to find the information you need. Before you can do this, however, you have to break down your research question or questions into key words and phrases. Let's suppose this was one of your research questions:

Was I entitled to an expert psychologist at my trial?

You can then break down this question into these key words and phrases: to psychologist

- Psychologist
- Mens Rea
- Intent (same as Mens Rea)
- Trial experts

Start with Secondary Sources

Almost all pro-se inmates jump directly to the CALR research which only serves to limit their intentions. Secondary resources are the best place to start all legal research. The best legal researchers (like I was trained to do) start with a legal encyclopedia, such as C.J.S. (Corpus Juris Secundum) and AM. Jur. 2d (American Jurisprudence 2d). I understand that some prison libraries will not have these. However, I have also discovered them in a few prison libraries as well. Federal inmates will absolutely have access to these publications. Also, in place, you can read a Treatise. Here you will find analyses and references to relevant cases.

When you are ready...move on to the primary resources.

Going to Primary Resources

Once you have a general idea of your legal 1ssues and area, you can move on to the following primary resources:

- Constitutions (federal and state)
- Statutes
- Cases
- Rules and Regulations

Now let's briefly break down what these things consist of, shall we?

1. Constitutions: In the previous chapters you learned that both the United States and individual states have constitutions. If you are in search of a case concerning the U.S. Constitution, you should consult the U.S.C.A. and U.S.C.S. Remember there are annotated versions of the U.S. Constitution that make it easier to read and understand. It also relates relevant cases which will be very helpful. If you need access to a state constitution, consult that state's annotated code.

2. Statutes: This is an absolute must. For federal statutes, check U.S.C.A. and U.S.C.S. Again, read the annotations.

3. Cases (Case Law): This is straight-forward. However, when you need more cases use digests and not just Shepardizing.

Enough is Enough

Legal research is a never-ending cycle; sources will lead you to more sources. Then those sources will lead you to even more sources. Seriously, stop the madness!

Knowing when to stop conducting research comes only with experience, and as you get better...you'll know better. When you have located some very strong and-binding authorities (maybe some persuasive as well), you are ready to present your arguments.

How to Read Case Law

When a judge makes a decision about a case, they will write a description of the facts of that case, the law they used in coming to their decision and the reason they came to their decision. That citing (case law) will have the following:

1. Summary: This is a short detail of facts related to the case.

2. Key Number Links: Directly under the summary, you might see the numbered paragraphs with headings and little pictures of keys. These are there to help you conduct research.

3. The Syllabus: This is a summary of the "holding" or decision in the case. This is never written by the judge so never cite it in your argument as an authority.

4. The Facts: Here the judges give you detailed information about the case that will help you determine if the case is similar to yours.

5. Legal Reasoning: Here the judges will provide you with past cases and standings that they used to determine this particular case.

6. The Holding: This is the actual decision of the judge and will help you determine if the case helps you or hurts you.

Citations

Every official decision has a "citation", which is the case name. The citation also explains what court made the decision and in what year. For example, this is a typical Supreme Court citation:

Johnson v. Avery (Name of the case)

The name of the case comes from the last name of the person bringing the suit and the last name of the person being sued. The name of the plaintiff always comes first at the trial level, but the names switch order after that since the plaintiff becomes the person defending at that point (At trial you are the defendant, but on appeal you are the appellant/plaintiff).

You should always italicize or underline the case name.

Johnson v. Avery, 393 U.S. 483, 485 (1969)

Here, the "393" is the number of the volume of United States Reports in which you can find the case.

The "U.S." indicates that the decision can be found in United States Reporters.

"483" is the page number in volume 393 on which the decision begins.

"1969" is the year the decision was announced.

Sometimes a U.S. Supreme Court decision will be cited to all three sets of reports, such as:

Johnson v. Avery, 393 U.S. 483, 89 S. Ct. 797, 21 L.Ed.2d 718 (1969).

You can cite all three if you want, but it's not usually required. The "U.S." part is the important part. Never give only the "S. Ct." or "L.Ed."

The "S. Ct", stands for "Supreme Court Reporter" and the "L.Ed." stands for "Lawyer's Edition". These books are supposed to be in your prison law library and usually give the "U.S." citation for each decision.

A typical Circuit Court citation is: (fictitious example)

Malachi v. Thaler, 123 F.3d 957, 958-59 (5th Cir. 2000)

This decision is in volume 123 of the Federal Reporter, third series, starting on page 957, continued on pages 958-59, in the year 2000.

Once you are able to read case law appropriately, you will be able to recall from memory those that are applicable to you. It's important that you know where to look and where to find cases that are binding on the Court.

The rest...is a matter of trial and error, along with repetition.

I wish you luck, success, and of course...relief.

Washington and Lee Law Review Online

Volume 74/Issue 1
Article 1

5-11-2017

An Indigent Criminal Defendant Is Entitled to "An Expert of His Own"

Fredrick E. Vars
University of Alabama School of Law

An Indigent Criminal Defendant Is Entitled to "An Expert of His Own"

Fredrick E. Vars*

Abstract

The Supreme Court recently heard the case of an Alabama death row inmate, James McWilliams. A thus far overlooked argument could save his life and help level the playing field in other capital cases. The Court in 1985 promised independent expertise. Now is its chance to make good on that promise.

---

*Professor, University of Alabama School of Law. Thanks to David Patton and Monique Fields for helpful comments on earlier drafts.

74 WASH. & LEE L. REV. ONLINE 1 (2017)

The Supreme Court recently heard arguments in the appeal of an Alabama death row inmate, James McWilliams.[1] An overlooked argument could save his life and help level the, playing field in other capital cases.

McWilliams was charged with rape and murder.[2] He could not afford a lawyer, so one was assigned to him by the court.[3] Before trial, his lawyer asked for and was granted a psychiatric evaluation.[4] McWilliams, on psychotropic medication at trial, was convicted.[5] Just two days prior to the judicial sentencing hearing, the state produced an expert report stating that McWilliams suffered from "cortical dysfunction attributable to right cerebral hemisphere dysfunction."[6]

At the hearing, McWilliams's attorney requested a continuance to get a second opinion from an independent expert, to understand. both the report and the voluminous, mental health records that were produced by the state at the last minute.[7] That request was denied.[8] As a result, McWilliams presented only his own and his mother's testimony during the sentencing phase.[9] Both described McWilliams's head trauma and poor mental health.[10] In rebuttal, the state presented its own experts' mental health testimony.[11] An aggravating factor is a prerequisite for a death sentence, so the state also offered evidence of three such factors, including a past felony conviction.[12] The judge sentenced McWilliams to death.[13]

The question presented now is whether a 1985 Supreme Court case, *Ake v. Oklahoma*,[14] clearly established that an indigent defendant who needs an expert is entitled to one who is

---

1. McWilliams v. Dunn, No. 16-5294 (S. Ct. argued Apr. 24, 2017).
2. Brief for Petitioner at 5, McWilliams v. Dunn, No. 16-5294 (S. Ct. Feb. 27, 2017), http://www.americanbar.org/content/dam/aba/publications/supreme_court_preview/briefs_2016_20 17/16-5294_ pet.authcheckdam.pdf.
3. *Id.*
4. *Id.*
5. *Id.*
6. *Id.* at 8.
7. *Id.* at 9.
8. *Id.*
9. *Id.* at 5.
10. *Id.* at 5-6.
11. *Id.* at 6.
12. *Id.* at 12.
13. *Id.*
14. 470 U.S. 68 (1985).

"AN EXPERT OF HIS OWN"

independent of the prosecution. The- parties have presented competing views of *Ake*,[15] which were thoroughly vetted at oral argument.[16]

McWilliams has the stronger argument. The motivating principle of *Ake* is to "assure- a proper functioning of the *adversary* process".[17] Consistent with that principle, *Ake* speaks of "psychiatrists for each party",[18] This is more than a passing reference. Later, the Court explained that the defense expert should "assist in preparing the cross-examination of a State's psychiatric witnesses".[19] This obviously makes no sense if the defense expert is also the state's expert. Clearly, the defense expert must be independent.[20]

This clarity is not diminished by *Ake's* statement that a defendant has no "constitutional right to choose a psychiatrist of his personal liking or to receive funds to hire his own."[21] Out of context, one might infer from this statement that defendants are not entitled to experts of their own. But the Court immediately slams the door on this inference, explaining that the right to an expert is analogous to the right to counsel.[22] Indigent defendants can obviously be assigned attorneys rather than be given money to hire one of their choosing.[23] Still, an assigned attorney must zealously and independently pursue the defendant's interests, not those of the prosecution.[24] A court retains the authority to deny funds for a particular expert, but not to deny an expert altogether.

---

15. *See generally* Brief for Petitioner, McWilliams v. Dunn, No. 16·5294 (S. Ct. Feb. 27, 2017); Brief for Respondent, McWilliams v. Dunn, No. 16-5294 (S. Ct. Mar. 29, 2017); *Reply Brief of Petitioner, McWilliams v. Dunn*, No. 16-5294 (S. Ct. Apr. 17, 2017). These briefs are available at http://www.americanbar.org/publications/preview_home/2016_2017_briefs/16- 5294.html.

16. *See generally* Transcript of Oral Argument, McWilliams v. Dunn, No. 16-5294 (S. Ct. 2017), https://www.supremecourt.gov/oral_arguments/argument_transcripts/2016/16-5294 _g314.pdf.

17. *Ake*, 470 U.S. at 77 (emphasis added).

18. *Id.* at 81.

19. *Id.* at 82.

20. *See* Carlton Bailey, Ake v. Oklahoma *and an Indigent Defendant's 'Right' to an Expert Witness: A Promise Denied or Imagined*, 10 WM. & MARY BILL RTS.J. 401, 458 (2002) (arguing that "courts which hold that *Ake* may be satisfied by a neutral expert ... misread *Ake*").

21. Ake v. Oklahoma, 470 U.S. 68, 83 (1985).

22. See *id.* at 76 (discussing the right to counsel as part of a defendant's right to meaningful access to justice).

23. See John M. West, *Expert Services and the Indigent Criminal Defendant: The Constitutional Mandate of* Ake v. Oklahoma, 84 MICH. L. REV. 1326, 1346 (1986) (arguing that "in all respects except the defendant's free choice of his expert, a 'partisan' expert is constitutionally required").

24. See Paul C. Giannelli, *The Right to Defense Experts*, 18 CRIM. JUST. 15, 18 (2003) (analogizing the right to a defense expert with the right to defense counsel).

74 WASH. & LEE L. REV. ONLINE 1 (2017)

But another strong argument for McWilliams remains hidden in plain sight. All the discussion above involves a defendant's right to an expert on the question of insanity in the guilt phase of trial. In a separate section, *Ake* left no doubt that an indigent criminal defendant is entitled to "an expert of his own" "when the State presents psychiatric evidence of the defendant's future dangerousness" during capital sentencing.[25] Allowing psychiatric evidence of future dangerousness, the Court explained, is premised on a defendant being able to present "the opposing views of the defendant's doctors" and "a well-informed expert's opposing view.[26] Moreover, the expert assistance for defendant is to include "assistance in preparation at the sentencing phase."[27]

There are good reasons the parties and the Court missed the relevance of this proposition for McWilliams. First, the state in *McWilliams* did not expressly assert future dangerousness.[28] But it no less injected future dangerousness into the case by introducing evidence of a prior felony conviction.[29] Felony convictions are often relied upon to establish future dangerousness,[30] and criminal history is a proxy for future offending.[31] The past felony convictions implied that McWilliams was, and would continue to be, a recidivist.

Second, future dangerousness was not a *statutory* aggravator in Alabama,[32] whereas it was in Oklahoma at the time of *Ake*.[33] This is a distinction without a difference. Whether future dangerousness appears in a statute or comes in by another path is irrelevant.[34] Either way (like a misdiagnosis in mitigation), it may determine whether a defendant lives or dies.

---

25. *Ake*, 470 U.S. at 83, 84; *cf.* Ralph Slovenko, *Post-Ake Developments on the Right to Psychiatric Assistance*, 23.J. PSYCHIATRY & L. 605, 613 (1995) ("Justice Marshall divided the *Ake* analysis to address separately the guilt and the sentencing phases of the trial.").

26. *Ake*, 470 U.S. at 84 (citations and internal quotation marks omitted); *see also* Roberson v. Director, TDCJ-CID, No. 2:09cv327, 2014 WL 5343198, at *23 (E.D. Tex. Sept. 30, 2014) ("Trial counsel presented a sound trial strategy on the issue of future dangerousness. He presented an expert to counter the State's experts and vigorously cross-examined the State's experts".).

27. *Ake*, 470 U.S. at 84.

28. *See generally* Brief for Petitioner, McWilliams v. Dunn, No. 16-5294 (S. Ct. Feb. 27, 2017).

29. *Id.* at 5.

30. *See, e.g.*, Atkins v. Virginia. 536 U.S, 304, 308 (2002) ("To prove future dangerousness, the State relied on [defendant's] prior felony convictions as well as the testimony of four victims of earlier robberies and assaults".).

31. BERNARD E. HARCOURT, AGAINST PREDICTION: PROFILING, POLICING, AND PUNISHING IN AN ACTUARIAL AGE 188 (2007).

32.   *See generally* ALA. CODE § 13A-5-49 (1975).

33.   Ake v, Oklahoma, 470 U.S. 68, 86 (1985).

34.   Buttrum v. Black, 721 F. Supp. 1268, 1311 n.9 (N.D. Ga. 1989) (discussing future dangerousness as an aggravating factor).

"AN EXPERT OF HIS OWN"

Third, the state did not rely initially on psychiatric evidence, but presented it only in rebuttal.[35] This distinction too is immaterial.[36] McWilliams's mental health was an issue well before sentencing and by far the most powerful mitigating factor. There was no doubt McWilliams would introduce mental health evidence, so the state had its mental health experts ready for rebuttal. Surely, the state cannot avoid *Ake* by reserving its psychiatric evidence for certain introduction later.

Fourth, the state's psychiatric evidence did not go directly to future dangerousness. Instead, the state used its experts to argue that Me Williams was faking his mental Illness.[37] That may seem like a significant distinction given *Ake's* focus on predicting future dangerousness.[38] But elsewhere the opinion recognizes that psychiatrists also "disagree widely and frequently on what constitutes mental illness" and "on the appropriate diagnosis to be attached to given behavior."[39] Detecting false symptoms is particularly difficult.[40] Expertise is as critical here, and the stakes are the same, as with future dangerousness.

When these factors are properly understood, it is even clearer *Ake* established that McWilliams was entitled to an independent expert.

Why are independent experts particularly important in capital sentencing? *Ake* explains that "[t]he State … has a profound interest in assuring that its ultimate sanction is not erroneously imposed".[41] In capital sentencing, mitigation evidence can directly tip the scale for or against death. Conviction of a crime, on the other hand, cannot lead automatically to a sentence of death.[42] Rather, a death sentence may be imposed only after consideration of all factors, including "the character   and   record   of   the   individual   offender."[43]   This   is   a

---

35.   Brief for Petitioner at 5, McWilliams v. Dunn, No. 16-5294 (S. Ct. Feb. 27,2017).

36.   *See* Castro v. Oklahoma, 71 F.3d 1502, 1514-1515 (10th Cir. 1995) (finding that the *Ake* duty to provide a defense expert is triggered anytime the State presents evidence of future dangerousness).

37.   Brief for Petitioner at 7, McWilliams v. Dunn, No. 16-5294 (S. Ct. Feb. 27, 2017).

38.   *See generally* Ake v. Oklahoma, 470 U.S. 68, 84 (1985).

39.   *Id*. at 81.

40.   *See* Phillip J. Resnick & James Knoll, Faking It: How to Detect Malingered Psychosis, 4 CURRENT PSYCHIATRY 12, 14 (2005) ("No other syndrome is as easy to define yet so difficult to diagnose as malingering".).

41.   *Ake*, 470 U.S. at 83-84; see also id. at 87 (Burger, C.J., concurring) ("In capital cases the finality of the sentence-imposed warrants protections that may or may not be required in other cases".).

42.   *See* Woodson v. North Carolina, 428 U.S. 280, 301 (1976) (finding that a mandatory death sentence statute violates the Eighth and Fourteenth Amendments).

43.   *Id*. at 304 (plurality opinion).

well-established constitutional requirement, whereas the Court has not decided whether the insanity defense is constitutionally required.[44]

These considerations indicate that the *Ake* duty to provide an independent expert should cover sentencing in every death penalty case.[45] The state should be required to provide a psychiatric expert even when future dangerousness is not squarely at issue. "[P]sychiatric testimony is generally of critical importance to the sentencing determination, covering issues of rehabilitative potential, future dangerousness, and individual culpability".[46] And not just psychiatric evidence is essential. In all capital cases, "because the defendant's medical, psychological, sociological, and family background must all be thoroughly investigated, counsel must seek out assistance from mitigation specialists".[47] Not providing indigent defendants this assistance thwarts their efforts to marshal mitigating evidence.

Another Supreme Court case, *Wiggins v. Smith*,[48] is instructive. In that case, the Court sustained a claim of ineffective assistance of counsel because the defense attorney failed to adequately investigate social history and therefore failed to uncover powerful evidence of sexual abuse.[49] One commentator correctly observed that, "[a]t a key point in its opinion, the Court chastised defense counsel for failing to 'commission' a social history report '[d]espite the fact that the Public Defender's office made funds available for the retention of a forensic social worker.'"[50] In other words, the Court instructed defense counsel to "commission" an expert report, not just rely on the state's expert. A constitutional duty to gather mitigating evidence is meaningful only if indigent defendants are provided with independent expert help.[51]

---

44. *See* Clark v. Arizona, 548 U.S. 735, 752 n.20 (2006) ("We have never held that the Constitution mandates an insanity defense, nor have we held that the Constitution does not so require".).

45. *See* Susan S. Brown, *After Ake: Implementing the Tools of an Adequate Defense*, 7 PACE L. REV. 201, 240-41 (1986) ("For psychiatric defense assistance at a capital sentencing proceeding, a defendant need not make the same threshold showing as must be made to obtain such assistance at trial.").

46. Satterwhite v. Texas, 86 U.S. 249, 264 (1988) (Marshall, J., concurring).

47. Craig M. Cooley, *Mapping the Monster's Mental Health and Social History: Why Capital Defense Attorneys and Public Defender Death Penalty Units Require the Services of Mitigation Specialists*, 30 OKLA. CITY U. L. REV. 23, 53 (2005); *cf.* Fredrick E. Vars, *Prosecutorial Misconduct: The Best Defense Is a Good Defense*, 73 WASH. & LEE L REV. ONLINE 465, 469 (2016) (arguing that "one key component of support should be mitigation specialists").

48. *539* U.S. 510 (2003).

49. *Id.* at 523-27.

50. *Constitutional Law*, 117 HARV. L. REV. 278, 284 (2003) (quoting *Wiggins*, 539 U.S. at 524).

51. *See id.* at 287 (arguing that *Ake* and *Wiggins* signal that "the Constitution requires the retention of mitigation specialists" in every capital sentencing).

"AN EXPERT OF HIS OWN"

Independent experts are especially important when mental health is involved. The Supreme Court has repeatedly recognized that mental health is relevant in death penalty cases.[52] But mental health evidence is more than just relevant in capital sentencing it is essential. The Court has held that the absence of an instruction informing the jury that it could consider as mitigating the defendant's mental condition, which arguably made him less culpable, violated the Eighth and Fourteenth Amendments.[53] The Court has also held that counsel's failure to uncover and present evidence of defendant's mental health at the penalty phase of a death penalty case was ineffective assistance of counsel.[54] Holding that mental health evidence is essential in mitigation without providing indigent defendants a genuine opportunity to uncover and present such evidence undermines the properly functioning "adversary process" that *Ake* is meant to protect.[55]

The Court in *Ake* promised independent expertise at least in capital sentencing. It has a chance now to make good on that promise, and perhaps save a life in the process.

---

52.   *See* Michael L. Perlin, *"Merchants and Thieves, Hungry for Power": Prosecutorial Misconduct and Passive Judicial Complicity in Death Penalty Trials of Defendants with Mental Disabilities*, 73 WASH. & LEE L. REV. 1501, 1501 (2016) (citing Hall v. Florida, 134 S. Ct. 1986 (2014); Panetti v. Quarterman, 551 U.S. 930 (2007); Atkins v. Virginia, 536 U.S. 304 (2002); Ford v. Wainwright, 477 U.S. 399 (1986)).

53.   Penry v. Lynaugh, 492 U.S. 302, 322-328 (1989), *rev'd on other grounds sub nom.* Atkins v. Virginia, 536 U.S. 304 (2002).

...54.   Porter v. McCollum, 558 U.S. 30, 38-40 (2009); *accord* Wiggins v. Smith, 539 U.S. 510 (2003).

55.   Ake v. Oklahoma, 470 U.S. 68, 77 (1985).

OCTOBER TERM, 2016

Syllabus

NOTE: Where it is feasible, a syllabus (headnote) will be released, as is being done in connection with this case, at the time the opinion if> issued. The syllabus constitutes no part of the opinion of the Court but has been prepared by the Reporter of Decisions for the convenience of the reader. See *United States v. Detroit Timber & Lumber Co.*, 200 U. S. 321, 337.

SUPREME COURT OF THE UNITED STATES

Syllabus

McWILLIAMS *v.* DUNN, COMMISSIONER, ALABAMA DEPARTMENT OF CORRECTIONS,

ET AL.

CERTIORARI TO THE UNITED STATES COURT OF APPEALS FOR THE ELEVENTH CIRCUIT

No. 16-5294. Argued April 24, 2017-Decided June 19, 2017

Ake v. Oklahoma, 470 U. S. 68, 83, clearly established that when an indigent "defendant demonstrates ... that his sanity at the time of the offense is to be a significant fact at trial, the State must" provide the defendant with "access to a competent psychiatrist who will conduct an appropriate examination and assist in evaluation, preparation, and presentation of the defense."

One month after Ake was decided, Alabama charged petitioner McWilliams with rape and murder. Finding him indigent, the trial court appointed counsel, who requested a psychiatric evaluation of McWilliams. The court granted the motion and the State convened a commission, which concluded that McWilliams was competent to stand trial and had not been suffering from mental illness at the time of the alleged offense. A jury convicted McWilliams of capital murder and recommended a death sentence. Later, while the parties awaited McWilliams' judicial sentencing hearing, McWilliams' counsel asked for neurological and neuropsychological testing of McWilliams. The court agreed and McWilliams was examined by Dr. Goff. Dr. Goff filed a report two days before the judicial sentencing hearing. He concluded that McWilliams was likely exaggerating his symptoms, but nonetheless appeared to have some genuine neuropsychological problems. Just before the hearing, counsel also received updated records from the commission's evaluation and previously subpoenaed mental health records from the Alabama Department of Corrections. At the hearing, defense counsel requested a continuance in order to evaluate all the new material and asked for the assistance of someone with expertise in psychological matters to review the findings. The trial court denied defense counsel's requests. At the conclusion of the hearing, the court sentenced McWilliams to death.

McWILLIAMS *v.* DUNN

Syllabus

On appeal, McWilliams argued that the trial court denied him the right to meaningful expert assistance guarantee by *Ake*. The Alabama Court of Criminal Appeals affirmed McWilliams' conviction and sentence, holding that Dr. Goff's examination satisfied *Ake's* requirements. The State Supreme Court affirmed, and McWilliams failed to obtain state postconviction relief. On federal habeas review, a Magistrate Judge also found that the Goff examination satisfied *Ake* and, therefore, that the State Court of Criminal Appeals' decision was not contrary to, or an unreasonable application of, clearly established federal law. See 28 U. S. C. §2254(d)(1). Adopting the Magistrate Judge's report and recommendation, the District Court denied relief. The Eleventh Circuit affirmed.

Held:

1. *Ake* clearly established that when certain threshold criteria are met, the state must provide a defendant with access to a mental health expert who is sufficiently available to the defense and independent from the prosecution to effectively "conduct an appropriate examination and assist in evaluation, preparation, and presentation of the defense." 470 U. S., at 83. The Alabama courts' determination that McWilliams received all the assistance to which *Ake* entitled him was contrary to, or an unreasonable application of, clearly established federal law.
Pp. 11-16.

(a) Three preliminary issues require resolution. First, the conditions that trigger *Ake's* application are present. McWilliams is and was an "indigent defendant," 470 U. S., at 70, and his "mental condition" was both "relevant to ... the punishment he might suffer," *id*, at 80, and "seriously in question," *id.*, at 70. Second, this Court rejects Alabama's claim the State was relieved of its *Ake* obligations because McWilliams received brief assistance from a volunteer psychologist at the University of Alabama. Even if the episodic help of an outside volunteer could satisfy *Ake*, the State does not refer to any specific record facts that indicate that the volunteer psychologist was available to the defense at the judicial sentencing proceeding. Third, contrary to Alabama's suggestion, the record indicates that McWilliams did not get all the mental health assistance that he requested. Rather, he asked for additional help at the judicial sentencing hearing but was rebuffed. Pp. 11-13.

(b) This Court does not have to decide whether *Ake* requires a State to provide an indigent defendant with a qualified mental health expert retained specifically for the defense team. That is because Alabama did not meet even *Ake's* most basic requirements in this case. *Ake* requires more than just an examination. It requires that the State provide the defense with "access to a competent psychiatrist who will conduct an appropriate [1] examination and assist in

Cite as: 582 U. S. ___ (2017)

Syllabus

[2] evaluation, [3] preparation, and [4] presentation of the defense". 470 U. S., at 83. Even assuming that Alabama met the examination requirement, it did not meet any of the other three. No expert helped the defense evaluate the Goff report or McWilliams' extensive medical records and translate these data into a legal strategy. No expert helped the defense prepare and present arguments that might, *e.g.*, have explained that McWilliams' purported malingering was not necessarily inconsistent with mental illness. No expert helped the defense prepare direct or cross-examination of any witnesses or testified at the judicial sentencing hearing. Since Alabama's provision of mental health assistance fell so dramatically short of Ake's requirements, the Alabama courts' decision affirming McWilliams' sentence was "contrary to, or involved an unreasonable application of, clearly established Federal law". 28 U. S. C. §2254(d)(1). Pp.13-16.

2. The Eleventh Circuit should determine on remand whether the Alabama courts' error had the "substantial and injurious effect or influence" required to warrant a grant of habeas relief, *Davis v, Ayala*, 576 U. S. ___, ___, specifically considering whether access to the type of meaningful assistance in evaluating, preparing, and presenting the defense that *Ake* requires could have made a difference. P. 16. 634 Fed. Appx. 698, reversed and remanded.

BREYER, J., delivered the opinion of the Court, in which KENNEDY, GINSBURG, SOTOMAYOR, and KAGAN, JJ., joined. ALITO, J., filed a dissenting opinion, in which ROBERTS, C. J., and THOMAS and GORSUCH, JJ., joined.

Cite as: 582 U. S. ___ (2017)

Opinion of the Court

NOTICE: This opinion is subject to formal revision before publication in the preliminary print of the United States Reports. Readers are requested to notify the Reporter of Decisions, Supreme Court of the United States, Washington, D. C. 20543, of any typographical or other formal errors, in order that corrections may be made before the preliminary print goes to press.

SUPREME COURT OF THE UNITED STATES

No. 16-5294

JAMES E. McWILLIAMS, PETITIONER *v.* JEFFERSON S. DUNN, COMMISSIONER, ALABAMA DEPARTMENT OF CORRECTIONS, ET AL.

ON WRIT OF CERTIORARI TO THE UNITED STATES COURT OF APPEALS FOR THE ELEVENTH CIRCUIT

[June 19, 2017]

JUSTICE BREYER delivered the opinion of the Court.

Thirty-one years ago, petitioner James Edmond McWilliams, Jr., was convicted of capital murder by an Alabama jury and sentenced to death. McWilliams challenged his sentence on appeal, arguing that the State had failed to provide him with the expert mental health assistance the Constitution requires, but the Alabama courts refused to grant relief. We now consider, in this habeas corpus case, whether the Alabama courts' refusal was "contrary to, or involved an unreasonable application of, clearly established Federal law". 28 U. S. C. §2254(d)(1). We hold that it was. Our decision in *Ake v. Oklahoma*, 470 U. S. 68 (1985), clearly established that, when certain threshold criteria are met, the State must provide an indigent defendant with access to a mental health expert who is sufficiently available to the defense and independent from the prosecution to effectively "assist in evaluation, preparation, and presentation of the defense." *Id.*, at 83. Petitioner in this case did not receive that assistance.

I

McWilliams and the State of Alabama agree that *Ake* (which this Court decided in February 1985) sets forth the applicable constitutional standards. Before turning to the circumstances of McWilliams' case, we describe what the Court held in *Ake*. We put in italics language that we find particularly pertinent here.

McWILLIAMS *v.* DUNN

Opinion of the Court

The Court began by stating that the "issue in this case is whether the Constitution requires that an indigent defendant have access to the psychiatric examination *and assistance necessary to prepare an effective defense based on his mental condition*, when his sanity at the time of the offense is seriously in question." *Id.*, at 70 (emphasis added). The Court said it would consider that issue within the framework of earlier cases granting "an indigent defendant ... a fair opportunity to present his defense" and "to participate meaningfully in a judicial proceeding in which his liberty is at stake". *Id.*, at 76. "Meaningful access to justice", the Court added, "has been the consistent theme of these cases". *Id.*, at 77.

The Court then wrote that "when the State has made the defendant's mental condition relevant to his criminal culpability and to the punishment he might suffer, the assistance of a psychiatrist may well be crucial to the defendant's ability to marshal his defense." *Id.*, at 80. A psychiatrist may, among other things, "gather facts", "analyze the information gathered and from it draw plausible conclusions", and "know the probative questions to ask of the opposing party's psychiatrists and how to interpret their answers". *Ibid.* These and related considerations

> "lea[d] inexorably to the conclusion that, *without the assistance of a psychiatrist to conduct a professional examination on issues relevant to the defense, to help determine whether the insanity defense is viable, to present testimony, and to assist in preparing the cross-examination of a State's psychiatric witnesses*, the risk of an inaccurate resolution of sanity issues is extremely high. With such assistance, the defendant is fairly able to present at least enough information to the jury, in a meaningful manner, as to permit it to make a sensible determination". *Id.*, at 82 (emphasis added).

The Court concluded; "We therefore hold that when a defendant demonstrates to the trial judge that his sanity at the time of the offense is to be a significant factor at trial, the State must, at a minimum, assure the defendant access to a competent psychiatrist who will conduct an appropriate examination and *assist in evaluation, preparation, and presentation of the defense* ... Our concern is that the indigent defendant has access to a competent psychiatrist *for the[se] purpose[s]*". *Id.*, at 83 (emphasis added).

Opinion of the Court

Ake thus clearly establishes that when its threshold criteria are met, a State must provide a mental health professional capable of performing a certain role: "conduct[ing] an appropriate examination and assist[ing] in evaluation, preparation, and presentation of the defense." *Ibid.* Unless a defendant is "assure[d]" the assistance of someone who can effectively perform these functions, he has not received the "minimum" to which *Ake* entitles him. *Ibid.*

II

A

One month after this Court decided *Ake*, the State of Alabama charged McWilliams with rape and murder. The trial court found McWilliams indigent and provided him with counsel. It also granted counsel's pretrial motion for a psychiatric evaluation of McWilliams' sanity, including aspects of his mental condition relevant to "mitigating circumstances to be considered in a capital case in the sentencing stage". T. 1526. ("T." refers to the certified trial record; "P. C. T." refers to the certified court reporter's state post-conviction proceedings transcript.) The court ordered the State to convene a "Lunacy Commission", which would examine McWilliams and file a report with the court. See *id.*, at 1528-1529.

Subsequently a three-member Lunacy Commission examined McWilliams at a state hospital, the Taylor Hardin Secure Medical Facility. The three members, all psychiatrists, concluded that McWilliams was competent to stand trial and that he had not been suffering from mental illness at the time of the alleged offense. *Id.*, at 1544-1546. One of them, Dr. Kamal Nagi, wrote that "Mr. McWilliams is grossly exaggerating his psychological symptoms to mimic mental illness". *Id.*, at 1546. Dr. Nagi noted that McWilliams' performance on one of the tests "suggested that [McWilliams] had exaggerated his endorsement of symptoms of illness and the profile was considered a 'fake bad.'" *Ibid.*

McWilliams' trial took place in late August 1986. On August 26 the jury convicted him of capital murder. The prosecution sought the death penalty, which under then-applicable Alabama law required both a jury recommendation (with at least 10 affirmative votes) and a later determination by the judge. See Ala. Code §13A-5-46(f) (1986). The jury-related portion of the

McWILLIAMS *v.* DUNN

Opinion of the Court

sentencing proceeding took place the next day. The prosecution reintroduced evidence from the guilt phase and called a police officer to testify that McWilliams had a prior conviction. T. 1297, 1299-1303. The defense called McWilliams and his mother. Both testified that McWilliams, when a child, had suffered multiple serious head injuries. *Id.*, at 1303-1318, 1320-1335. McWilliams also described his history of psychiatric and psychological evaluations, reading from the prearrest report of one psychologist, who concluded that McWilliams had a "blatantly psychotic thought disorder" and needed inpatient treatment. *Id.*, at 1329-1332.

When the prosecutor, cross-examining McWilliams, asked about the neurological effects of his head injuries, McWilliams replied, "I am not a psychiatrist". *Id.*, at 1328. Similarly, when the prosecutor asked McWilliams' mother whether her son was "crazy", she answered, "I am no expert: I don't know whether my son is crazy or not. All I know that my son does need help". *Id.*, at 1317.

The prosecution then called two of the mental health professionals who had signed the Lunacy Commission's report, Dr. Kamal Nagi and Dr. Norman Poythress. Dr. Nagi testified that he had found no evidence of psychosis but did not appear to be aware of McWilliams' history of head trauma. See *id.*, at 1351-1352. Dr. Poythress testified that one of the tests that McWilliams took was "clinically invalid" because the test's "validity scales" indicated that McWilliams had exaggerated or faked his symptoms. *Id.*, at 1361-1363.

Although McWilliams' counsel had subpoenaed further mental health records from Holman State Prison, where McWilliams was being held, the jury did not have the opportunity to consider them, for, though subpoenaed on August 13, the records had not arrived by August 27, the day of the jury hearing.

After the hearing, the jury recommended the death penalty by a vote of 10 to 2, the minimum required by Alabama law. The court scheduled its judicial sentencing hearing for October 9, about six weeks later.

B

Five weeks before that hearing, the trial court ordered the Alabama Department of Corrections to respond to McWilliams's subpoena for mental health records. *Id.*, at 1619. The court also granted McWilliams' motion for neurological and neuropsychological exams. *Id.*, at 1615-1617. That motion (apparently filed at the suggestion of a University of Alabama psychologist who had "volunteer[ed]" to help counsel "in her spare time," P. C. T. 251- 252) asked the court to "issue an order requiring the State of Alabama to do complete neurological and neuropsychological testing on the Defendant in order to have the test results available for his sentencing hearing." T. 1615.

Consequently, Dr. John Goff, a neuropsychologist employed by the State's Department of Mental Health, examined McWilliams. On October 7, two days before the judicial sentencing hearing, Dr. Goff filed his report. The report concluded that McWilliams presented "some diagnostic dilemmas". *Id.*, at 1635. On the one hand, he was "obviously attempting to appear emotionally disturbed" and "exaggerating his neuropsychological problems". *Ibid.* But on the other hand, it was "quite apparent that he ha[d] some genuine neuropsychological problems". *Ibid.* Tests revealed "cortical dysfunction attributable to right cerebral hemisphere dysfunction", shown by "left hand weakness, poor motor coordination of the left hand, sensory deficits including suppressions of the left hand and very poor visual search skills". *Id.*, at 1636. These deficiencies were "suggestive of a right hemisphere lesion" and "compatible with the injuries [McWilliams] sa[id] he sustained as a child". *Id.*, at 1635. The report added that McWilliams' "obvious neuropsychological deficit" could he related to his "low frustration tolerance and impulsivity" and suggested a diagnosis of "organic personality syndrome". *Ibid.*

The day before the sentencing hearing defense counsel also received updated records from Taylor Hardin hospital, and on the morning of the hearing he received the records (subpoenaed in mid-August) from Holman Prison. The prison records indicated that McWilliams was taking an assortment of psychotropic medications including Desyrel, Librium, and an antipsychotic, Mellaril. See App. 190a-193a.

McWILLIAMS *v.* DUNN

Opinion of the Court

C

The judicial sentencing hearing began on the morning of October 9. Defense counsel told the trial court that the eleventh-hour arrival of the Goff report and the mental health records left him "unable to present any evidence today". *Id.*, at 194a. He said he needed more time to go over the new information. Furthermore, since he was "not a psychologist or a psychiatrist", he needed "to have someone else review these findings" and offer "a second opinion as to the severity of the organic problems discovered". *Id.*, at 192a-196a.

The trial judge responded, "All right. Well, let's proceed". *Id.*, at 197a. The prosecution then presented its case. Once it had finished, defense counsel moved for a continuance in order "to allow us to go through the material that has been provided to us in the last 2 days". *Id.*, at 204a. The judge offered to give defense counsel until 2 p.m. that afternoon. He also stated that "[a]t that time, The Court will entertain any motion that you may have with some other person to review" the new material. *Id.*, at 205a. Defense counsel protested that "there is no way that I can go through this material", but the judge immediately added, "Well, I will give you the opportunity ... If you do not want to try, then you may not". *Id.*, at 206a. The court then adjourned until 2 p.m.

During the recess, defense counsel moved to withdraw. He said that "the arbitrary [sic] position taken by this Court regarding the Defendant's right to present mitigating circumstances is unconscionable resulting in this proceeding being a mockery". T. 1644. He added that "further participation would be tantamount to acceptance [sic] of the Court's ruling". *Ibid.* The trial court denied the motion to withdraw.

When the proceedings resumed, defense counsel renewed his motion for a continuance, explaining,

"It is the position of the Defense that we have received these records at such a late date, such a late time that it has put us in a position as laymen, with regard to psychological matters, that we cannot adequately make a determination as what to present to The Court with regards to the particular deficiencies that the Defendant has. We believe that he has the type of diagnosed illness that we pointed out earlier for The Court and have mentioned for The Court. But we cannot determine ourselves from the records that we have received and the lack of receiving the test and the lack of our own expertise, whether or not such a condition exists; whether the reports and tests that have been run by Taylor Hardin, and the Lunacy Commission, and at Holman are tests that should be challenged in some type of way or the results should be challenged, we really need an opportunity to have the right type of experts in this field, take a look at all of those records and tell us what is happening with him. And that is why we renew the Motion for a Continuance". App, 207a.

The trial court denied the motion.

The prosecutor then offered his closing statement, in which he argued that there were "no mitigating circumstances". *Id.*, at 209a. Defense counsel replied that he "would be pleased to respond to [the prosecutor's] remarks that there are no mitigating circumstances in this case if I were able to have time to produce ... any mitigating circumstances". *Id.*, at 210a. But, he said, since neither he nor his co-counsel were "doctors", neither was "really capable of going through those records on our own". *Ibid.* The court had thus "foreclosed by structuring this hearing as it has, the Defendant from presenting any evidence of mitigation in psychological-psychiatric terms". *Id.*, at 211a.

The trial judge then said that he had reviewed the records himself and found evidence that McWilliams was faking and manipulative. *Ibid.* Defense counsel attempted to contest that point, which led to the following exchange:

> "MR. SOGOL: I told Your Honor that my looking at those records was not of any value to me; that I needed to have somebody look at those records who understood them, who could interpret them for me. Did I not tell Your Honor that?
>
> THE COURT: As I said, on the record earlier, Mr. Sogol, and I don't want to argue or belabor this, but I would have given you the opportunity to make a motion to present someone to evaluate that.
>
> MR. SOGOL: Your Honor gave me no time in which to do that. Your Honor told me to be here at 2 o'clock this afternoon. Would Your Honor have wanted me to file a Motion for Extraordinary Expenses to get someone?
>
> THE COURT: I want you to approach with your client, please". *Id.*, at 211a-212a.

The court then sentenced McWilliams to death.

McWILLIAMS *v.* DUNN

Opinion of the Court

The court later issued a written sentencing order. It found three aggravating circumstances and no mitigating circumstances. It found that McWilliams "was not and is not psychotic", and that "the preponderance of the evidence from these tests and reports show [McWilliams] to be feigning, faking, and manipulative". *Id.*, at 188a. The court wrote that even if McWilliams' mental health issues "did rise to the level of a mitigating circumstance, the aggravating circumstances would far outweigh this as a mitigating circumstance". *Ibid.*

D

McWilliams appealed, arguing that the trial court had denied him the right to meaningful expert assistance guaranteed by *Ake*. The Alabama Court of Criminal Appeals rejected his argument. It wrote that *Ake's* requirements "are met when the State provides the [defendant] with a competent psychiatrist". *McWilliams v. State*, 640 So. 2d 982, 991 (1991). And Alabama, by "allowing Dr. Goff to examine" McWilliams, had satisfied those requirements. *Ibid.* The court added that "[t]here is no indication in the record that [McWilliams] could not have called Dr. Goff as witness to explain his findings or that he even tried to contact the psychiatrist to discuss his findings," *ibid.*; that "the trial court indicated that it would have considered a motion to present an expert to evaluate this report" had one been made, *ibid.*; and that there was "no prejudice by the court's denial of [McWilliams'] motion for continuance," *id* at 993. The appeals court therefore affirmed McWilliams' conviction and sentence. The Alabama Supreme Court, in turn, affirmed the appeals court (without addressing the *Ake* issue). *Ex parte McWilliams*, 640 So. 2d 1015 (1993), After McWilliams failed to obtain postconviction relief from state courts, he sought a federal writ of habeas corpus. See 28 U. S. C. §2254.

E

In federal habeas court McWilliams argued before a Magistrate Judge that he had not received the expert assistance that *Ake* required. The Magistrate Judge recommended against issuing the writ. He wrote that McWilliams had "received the assistance required by *Ake*" because Dr. Goff "completed the testing" that McWilliams requested. App. 88a. Hence, the decision of the Alabama Court of Criminal Appeals was not contrary to, or an unreasonable application of, clearly established federal law. See 28 U. S. C. §2254(d)(1). The District Court adopted the Magistrate Judge's report and recommendation and denied relief. A divided panel of the Eleventh Circuit Court of Appeals affirmed. See *McWilliams v. Commissioner, Ala. Dept. of Corrections*, 634 Fed. Appx, 698 (2015) (*per curiam*); *id.*, at 711 (Jordan, J., concurring); *id.*, at 712 (Wilson, J., dissenting).

McWilliams filed a petition for certiorari. We granted the petition.

Cite as: 582 U. S.___ (2017)

Opinion of the Court

III

A

The question before us is whether the Alabama Court of Criminal Appeals' determination that McWilliams got all the assistance to which *Ake* entitled him was "contrary to, or involved an unreasonable application of, clearly established Federal law." 28 U. S. C. §2254(d)(1). Before turning to the heart of that question, we resolve three preliminary issues.

First, no one denies that the conditions that trigger application of *Ake* are present. McWilliams is and was an "indigent defendant", 470 U.S., at 70. See *supra*, at 3. His "mental condition" was "relevant to ... the punishment he might suffer", 470 U.S., at 80. See *supra*, at 4-5. And, that "mental condition", *i.e.;* his "sanity at the time of the offense", was "seriously in question", 470 U. S., at 70. See *supra*, at 4-5. Consequently, the Constitution, as interpreted in *Ake*, required the State to provide McWilliams with "access to a competent psychiatrist who will conduct an appropriate examination and assist in evaluation, preparation, and presentation of the defense". 470 U.S., at 83.

Second, we reject Alabama's claim that the State was exempted from its obligations because McWilliams already had the assistance of Dr. Rosenzweig, the psychologist at the University of Alabama who "volunteer[ed]" to help defense counsel "in her spare time" and suggested the defense ask for further testing, P. C. T. 251-252. Even if the episodic assistance of an outside volunteer could relieve the State of its constitutional duty to ensure an indigent defendant access to meaningful expert assistance, no lower court has held or suggested that Dr. Rosenzweig was available to help, or might have helped, McWilliams at the judicial sentencing proceeding, the- proceeding here at issue. Alabama does not refer to any specific record facts that indicate that she was available to the defense at this time.

Third, Alabama argues that *Ake's* requirements are irrelevant because McWilliams "never asked for more expert assistance" than he got, "even though the trial court gave him the opportunity to do so". Brief for Respondent 50-51. The record does not support this contention. When defense counsel requested a continuance at the sentencing hearing, he repeatedly told the court that he needed "to have someone else review" the Goff report and medical records. App. 193a. See, *e.g.*, *id.*, at 196a ("[I]t is just incumbent upon me to have a second opinion as to the severity of the organic problems discovered"); *id.*, at 207a ("[W]e really need an opportunity to have the right type of experts in this field, take a look at all of these records and tell us what is happening with him"); *id.*, at 211a ("I told Your Honor that my looking at these records was not of any value to me; that I needed to have somebody look at those records who understood them, who could interpret them for me"). Counsel also explicitly asked the trial court what else he was supposed to ask for to obtain an expert: "Would Your Honor have wanted me to file a Motion for Extraordinary Expenses to get someone?" *Id.*, at 212a. We have reproduced a lengthier account

McWILLIAMS *v.* DUNN

Opinion of the Court

of the exchanges, *supra*, at 7-9. They make clear that counsel wanted additional expert assistance to review the report and records-that was the point of asking for a continuance. In response, the court told counsel to approach the bench and sentenced McWilliams to death. Thus, the record, in our view, indicates that McWilliams did request additional help from mental health experts.

B

We turn to the main question before us: whether the Alabama Court of Criminal Appeals' determination that McWilliams got all the assistance that *Ake* requires was "contrary to, or involved an unreasonable application of, clearly established Federal law." 28 U. S. C. §2254(d)(1).

McWilliams would have us answer "yes" on the ground that *Ake* clearly established that a State must provide an indigent defendant with a qualified mental health expert retained specifically for the defense team, not a neutral expert available to both parties. He points to language in *Ake* that seems to foresee that consequence. See, *e.g.*, 470 U.S., at 81 ("By organizing a defendant's mental history, examination results and behavior, and other information, interpreting it in light of their expertise, and then laying out their investigative and analytic process to the jury, *the psychiatrists for each party* enable the jury to make its most accurate determination of the truth on the issue before them" (emphasis added)).

We need not, and do not, decide, however, whether this particular McWilliams claim is correct. As discussed above, *Ake* clearly established that a defendant must receive the assistance of a mental health expert who is sufficiently available to the defense and independent from the prosecution to effectively "assist in evaluation, preparation, and presentation of the defense". *Id.*, at 83. As a practical matter, the simplest way for a State to meet this standard may be to provide a qualified expert retained specifically for the defense team. This appears to be the approach that the overwhelming majority of jurisdictions have adopted. See Brief for National Association of Criminal Defense Lawyers et al. as *Amici Curiae* 8-35 (describing practice in capital-active jurisdictions); Tr. of Oral Arg, 40 (respondent conceding that "this issue really has been mooted over the last 30-some-odd years because of statutory changes"). It is not necessary, however, for us to decide whether the Constitution requires States to satisfy *Ake's* demands in this way. That is because Alabama here did not meet even *Ake's* most basic requirements.

The dissent calls our unwillingness to resolve the broader question whether *Ake* clearly established a right to an expert independent from the prosecution a "most unseemly maneuver".

Cite as: 582 U. S. __ (2017)

Opinion of the Court

Post, at 1-2 (opinion of ALITO, J.). We do not agree. We recognize that we granted petitioner's first question presented-which addressed whether *Ake* clearly established a right to an independent expert-and not his second, which raised more case-specific concerns. See Pet. for Cert. i. Yet that does not bind us to issue a sweeping ruling when a narrow one will do. As we explain below, our determination that *Ake* clearly established that a defendant must receive the assistance of a mental health expert who is sufficiently available to the defense and independent from the prosecution to effectively "assist in evaluation, preparation, and presentation of the defense," 470 U.S., at 83, is sufficient to resolve the case. We therefore need not decide whether *Ake* clearly established more. (Nor do we agree with the dissent that our approach is "acutely unfair to Alabama" by not "giv[ing] the State a fair chance to respond". *Post*, at 12. In fact, the State devoted an entire section of its merits brief to explaining why it thought that "[n]o matter how the Court resolves the [independent expert] question, the court of appeals correctly denied the habeas petition". Brief for Respondent 50. See also *id*, at 14, 52 (referring to the lower courts' case-specific determinations that McWilliams got all the assistance *Ake* requires)).

The Alabama appeals court held that "the requirements of *Ake v. Oklahoma* ... are met when the State provides the [defendant] with a competent psychiatrist. The State met this requirement in allowing Dr. Goff to examine [McWilliams]". *McWilliams*, 640 So. 2d, at 991. This was plainly incorrect. *Ake* does not require just an examination. Rather, it requires the State to provide the defense with "access to a competent psychiatrist who will conduct an appropriate [1] *examination* and assist in [2] *evaluation*, [3] *preparation*, and [4] *presentation* of the defense". *Ake, supra,* at 83 (emphasis added).

We are willing to assume that Alabama met the *examination* portion of this requirement by providing for Dr. Goff's examination of McWilliams. See *supra,* at 6. But what about the other three parts? Neither Dr. Goff nor any other expert helped the defense evaluate Goff's report or McWilliams' extensive medical records and translate these data into a legal strategy. Neither Dr. Goff nor any other expert helped the defense prepare and present arguments that might, for example, have explained that McWilliams' purported malingering was not necessarily inconsistent with mental illness (as an expert later testified in postconviction proceedings, see P. C. T. 936-943). Neither Dr. Goff nor any other expert helped the defense prepare direct or cross-examination of any witnesses or testified at the judicial sentencing hearing himself.

The dissent emphasizes that Dr. Goff was never ordered to do any of these things by the trial court. See *post,* at 13, n. 5. But that is precisely the point. The relevant court order did not ask Dr. Goff or anyone else to provide the defense with help in evaluating, preparing, and presenting

McWILLIAMS *v.* DUNN

Opinion of the Court

its case. It only required "the Department of Corrections" to "complete neurological and neuropsychological testing on the Defendant ... and send all test materials, results and evaluations to the Clerk of the Court". T. 1612. Nor did the short time frame allow for more expert assistance. (Indeed, given that time frame, we do not see how Dr. Goff, or any other expert could have satisfied the latter three portions of *Ake's* requirements even had he been instructed to do so.) Then, when McWilliams asked for the additional assistance to which he was constitutionally entitled at the sentencing hearing, the judge rebuffed his requests. See *supra, at 7-9.*

Since Alabama's provision of mental health assistance fell so dramatically short of what *Ake* requires, we must conclude that the Alabama court decision affirming McWilliams's conviction and sentence was "contrary to, or involved an unreasonable application of, clearly established Federal law." 28 U. S. C. §2254(d)(1).

IV

The Eleventh Circuit held in the alternative that, even if the Alabama courts clearly erred in their application of federal law, their "error" nonetheless did not have the "substantial and injurious effect or influence" required to warrant a grant of habeas relief, *Davis* v. *Ayala*, 576 U.S. __, __ (2015) (slip op., at 10) (internal quotation marks omitted). See 634 Fed. Appx., at 707. In reaching this conclusion, however, the Eleventh Circuit only considered whether "[a] few additional days to review Dr. Goff's findings" would have made a difference. *Ibid.* It did not specifically consider whether access to the type of meaningful assistance in evaluating, preparing, and presenting the defense that *Ake* requires would have mattered. There is reason to think that it could have. For example, the trial judge relied heavily on his belief that McWilliams was malingering. See App. 188a, 211a. If McWilliams had the assistance of an expert to explain that "[m]alingering is not inconsistent with serious mental illness", Brief for American Psychiatric Association et al. as *Amici Curiae* 20, he might have been able to alter the judge's perception of the case.

Since "we are a court of review, not of first view", *Cutter* v. *Wilkinson*, 544 U. S. 709, 718, n. 7 (2005), we do not now resolve this question. Rather we leave it to the lower courts to decide in the first instance.

The judgment of the Court of Appeals is reversed, and the case is remanded for further proceedings consistent with this opinion.

It is so ordered.

U.S. Code Titles

Title 1: General Provisions

Title 2: The Congress

Title 3: The President

Title 4: Flag and Seal, Seat of Government, And the States

Title 5: Government Organization and Employees

Title 5a: Federal Advisory Committee Act

Title 6: Domestic Security

Title 7: Agriculture

Title 8: Aliens and Nationality

Title 9: Arbitration

Title 10: Armed Forces

Title 11: Bankruptcy

Title 11a: Bankruptcy Rules

Title 12: Banks and Banking

Title 13: Census

Title 14: Coast Guard

Title 15: Commerce and Trade

Title 16: Conservation

Title 17: Copyrights

Title 18: Crimes and Criminal Procedure

Title 18a: Unlawful Possession or Receipt of Firearms

Title 19: Customs Duties

Title 20: Education

Title 21: Food and Drugs

Title 22: Foreign Relations and Intercourse

Title 23: Highways

Title 24: Hospitals and Asylums

Title 25: Indians

Title 26: Internal Revenue Code

Title 27: Intoxicating Liquors

Title 28: Judiciary and Judicial Procedure

Title 28a: Judicial Personnel Financial Disclosure Requirements

Title 29: Labor

Title 30: Mineral Lands and Mining

Title 31: Money and Finance

Title 32: National Guard

Title 33: Navigation and Navigable Waters

Title 34: Crime Control and Law Enforcement

Title 35: Patents

Title 36: Patriotic and National Observances, Ceremonies, and Organizations

Title 37: Pay and Allowances of The Uniformed Services

Title 38: Veterans' Benefits

Title 39: Postal Service

Raymond E. Lumsden

Title 40: Public Buildings, Property, and Works

Title 41: Public Contracts

Title 42: The Public Health and Welfare

Title 43: Public Lands

Title 44: Public Printing and Documents

Title 45: Railroads

Title 46: Shipping

Title 47: Telecommunications

Title 48: Territories and Insular Possessions

Title 49: Transportation

Title 50: War and National Defense

Title 50a: War and National Defense [Eliminated] Current Through 114–86u1

Title 51: National and Commercial Space Programs

Title 52: Voting and Elections

Title 53: [Reserved]

Title 54: National Park Service and Related Programs

Glossary

Acquittal: A jury verdict that a criminal defendant is not guilty, or the finding of a judge that the evidence is insufficient to support a conviction.

Active judge: A judge in the full-time service of the court. Compare to senior judge.

Administrative Office of the United States Courts (AO): The federal agency responsible for collecting court statistics, administering the federal courts' budget, and performing many other administrative and programmatic functions, under the direction and supervision of the Judicial Conference of the United States.

Admissible: A term used to describe evidence that may be considered by a jury or judge in civil and criminal cases.

Affidavit: A written, or printed statement made under oath.

Affirmed: In the practice of the court of appeals, it means that the court of appeals has concluded that the lower court decision is correct and will stand as rendered by the lower court.

Alternate juror: A juror selected in the same manner as a regular juror who hears all the evidence but does not help decide the case unless called on to replace a regular juror.

Amicus curiae: "Latin for friend of the court". It is advice formally offered to the court in a brief filed by an entity interested in, but not a party to, the case.

Answer: The formal written statement by a defendant in a civil case that responds to a complaint, articulating the grounds for defense.

Appeal: A request made after a trial by a party that has lost on one or more issues that a higher court review the decision to determine if it was correct. To make such a request is "to appeal" or "to take an appeal". One who appeals is called the "appellant", the other party is the "appellee".

Appellant: The party who appeals a district court's decision, usually seeking reversal of that decision,

Appellate: About appeals; an appellate court has the power to review the judgment of a lower court (trial court) or tribunal. For example, the U.S. circuit courts of appeals review the decisions of the U.S. district courts.

Appellee: The party who opposes an appellant's appeal, and who seeks to persuade the appeals court to affirm the district court's decision.

Arraignment: A proceeding in which a criminal defendant is brought into court, told of the charges in an indictment or information, and asked to plead guilty or not guilty.

Article III judge: A federal judge who is appointed for life, during "good behavior", under Article III of the Constitution. Article III judges are nominated by the President and confirmed by the Senate.

Bail: The release, prior to trial, of a person accused of a crime, under specified conditions designed to assure that person's appearance in court when required. Also, can refer to the amount of bond money posted as a financial condition of pretrial release.

Bench trial: A trial without a jury, in which the judge serves as the fact finder.

Brief: A written statement submitted in a trial or appellate proceeding that explains one side's legal and factual arguments.

Burden of proof: The duty to prove disputed facts. In civil cases, a plaintiff generally has the burden of proving his or her case. In criminal cases, the government has the burden of proving the defendant's guilt. (See standard of proof.)

Capital offense: A crime punishable by death.

Case file: A complete collection of every document filed in court in a case.

Case law: The law as established in previous court decisions. A synonym for legal precedent. Akin to common law, which springs from tradition and judicial decisions.

Caseload: The number of cases handled by a judge or a court.

Cause of action: A legal claim.

Chambers: The offices of a judge and his or her staff.

Chief judge: The judge who has primary responsibility for the administration of a court, chief judges are determined by seniority.

Clerk of court: The court officer who oversees administrative functions, especially managing the flow of cases through the court. The clerk's office is often called a court's central nervous system.

Complaint: A written statement that begins a civil lawsuit, in which the plaintiff details the claims against the defendant.

Concurrent sentence: Prison terms of two or more offenses to be served at the same time, rather than one after the other. Example: Two five-year sentences and one three-year sentence, if served concurrently, result in a maximum of five years behind bars.

Consecutive sentence: Prison terms for two or more offenses to be served one after the other. Example: Two five-year sentences and one three-year sentence, if served consecutively, result in a maximum of 13 years behind bars.

Conviction: A judgment of guilt against a criminal defendant.

Counsel: Legal advice, a term also used to refer to the lawyers in a cast.

Count: An allegation in an indictment or information, charging a defendant with a crime. An indictment or information may contain allegations that the defendant committed more than one crime. Each allegation is referred to as a count.

Court: Government entity authorized to resolve legal disputes. Judges sometimes use "court" to refer to themselves in the third person, as in "the court has read the "briefs".

Court reporter: A person who makes a word-for-word record of what is said in court, generally by using a stenographic machine, shorthand or audio recording, and then produces a transcript of the proceedings upon request.

De facto: Latin, meaning "in fact" or "actually". Something that exists in fact but not as a matter of law.

De jure: Latin, meaning "in law". Something that exists by operation of law.

De novo: Latin, meaning "anew". A trial de novo is a completely new trial. Appellate review de novo implies no deference to the trial judge's ruling.

Defendant: In a civil case, the person or organization against whom the plaintiff brings suit; in a criminal case, the person accused of the crime.

Deposition: An oral statement made before an officer authorized by law to administer oaths. Such statements are often taken to examine potential witnesses, to obtain discovery, or to be used later in trial. See discovery.

Discovery: Procedures used to obtain disclosure of evidence before trial.

Dismissal with prejudice: Court action that prevents an identical lawsuit from being filed later.

Dismissal without prejudice: Court action that allows the later filing.

Docket: A log containing the complete history of each case in the form of brief chronological entries summarizing the court proceedings.

Due process: In criminal law, the constitutional guarantee that a defendant will receive a fair and impartial trial. In civil law, the legal rights of someone who confronts an adverse action threatening liberty or property.

En banc: French, meaning "on the bench". All judges of an appellate court sitting together to hear a case, as opposed to the routine disposition by panels of three judges. In the Ninth Circuit, an en banc panel consists of 11 randomly selected judges.

Evidence: Information presented in testimony or in documents that is used to persuade the fact finder (judge or jury) to decide the case in favor of one side or the other.

Ex parte: A proceeding brought before a court by one party only, without notice to or challenge by the other side.

Exculpatory evidence: Evidence indicating that a defendant did not commit the crime.

Federal public defender: An attorney employed by the federal courts on a full-time basis to provide legal defense to defendants who are unable to afford counsel. The judiciary administers the federal defender program pursuant to the Criminal Justice Act.

Federal public defender organization: As provided for in the Criminal Justice Act, an organization established within a federal judicial circuit to represent criminal defendants who cannot afford an adequate defense. Each organization is supervised by a federal public defender appointed by the court of appeals for the circuit.

Federal question jurisdiction: Jurisdiction given to federal courts in cases involving the interpretation and application of the U.S. Constitution, acts of Congress, and treaties.

Felony: A serious crime, usually punishable by at least one year in prison.

File: To place a paper in the official custody of the clerk of court to enter into the files or records of a case.

Grand jury: A body of 16-23 citizens who listen to evidence of criminal allegations, which is presented by the prosecutors, and determine whether there is probable cause to believe an individual committed an offense. See also indictment and U.S. attorney.

Habeas corpus: Latin, meaning "you have the body". A writ of habeas corpus generally is a judicial order forcing law enforcement authorities to produce a prisoner they are holding, and to justify the prisoner's continued confinement. Federal judges receive petitioners for a writ of habeas corpus from state prison inmates who say their state prosecutions violated federally protected rights in some way.

Inculpatory evidence: Evidence indicating that a defendant did commit a crime.

Indictment: The formal charge issued by a grand jury stating that there is enough evidence that the defendant committed the crime to justify having a trial; it is used primarily for felonies. See also information.

Information: A formal accusation by a government attorney that the defendant committed a misdemeanor. See also Indictment.

Interrogatories: A form of discovery consisting of written questions to be answered in writing and under oath.

Issue: 1. The disputed point between parties in a lawsuit; 2. To send out officially, as in a court issuing an order.

Judge: An official of the Judicial branch with authority to decide lawsuits brought before courts. Used generally, the term judge may also refer to all judicial officers, including Supreme Court justices.

Judgeship: The position of judge. By statute, Congress authorizes the number of judgeships for each district and appellate court.

Judgment: The official decision of a court finally resolving the dispute between the parties to the lawsuit.

Jurisprudence: The study of law and the structure of the legal system.

Jury: The group of persons selected to hear the evidence in a trial

Magistrate judge: A judicial officer of a district court who conducts initial proceedings in criminal cases, decides criminal misdemeanor cases, conducts many pretrial civil and criminal matters on behalf of district judges, and decides civil cases with the consent of the parties.

Mental health treatment: Special condition the court imposes to require an individual to undergo evaluation and treatment for a mental disorder. Treatment may include psychiatric, psychological, and sex offense-specific evaluations, inpatient or outpatient counseling, and medication.

Misdemeanor: An offense punishable by one year of imprisonment or less. See felony.

Moot: Not subject to a court ruling because the controversy has not actually arisen or has ended.

Opinion: A judge's written explanation of the decision of the court. Because a case may be heard by three or more judges in the court of appeals, the opinion in appellate decisions can take several forms. If all the judges completely agree on the result, one judge will write the opinion for all. If all the judges do not agree, the formal decision will be based upon the view of the majority, and one member of the majority will write the opinion. The judges who did not agree with the majority may write separately in dissenting or concurring opinions to present their views. A dissenting opinion disagrees with the majority opinion because of the reasoning and/or the principles of law the majority used to decide the case. A concurring opinion agrees with the decision of the majority opinion but offers further comment or clarification or even an entirely different reason for reaching the same result. Only the majority opinion can serve as binding precedent in future cases. See also precedent.

Oral argument: An opportunity for lawyers to summarize their position before the court and also to answer the judges' questions.

Per curiam: Latin, meaning "for the court". In appellate courts, often refers to an unsigned opinion.

Plaintiff: A person or business that files a formal complaint with the court.

Precedent: A court decision in an earlier case with facts and legal issues similar to a dispute currently before a court. Judges will generally "follow precedent" – meaning that they use the principles established in earlier cases to decide new cases that have similar facts and raise similar legal issues. A judge will disregard precedent if a party can show that the earlier case was wrongly decided, or that it differed in some significant way from the current case.

Pro se: Representing oneself. Serving as one's own lawyer.

Prosecute: To charge someone with a crime. A prosecutor tries a criminal case on behalf of the government.

Record: A written account of the proceedings in a case, including all pleadings, evidence, and exhibits submitted in the course of the case.

Remand: Send back.

Reverse: The act of a court setting aside the decision of a lower court. A reversal is often accompanied by a remand to the lower court for further proceedings.

Sentence: The punishment ordered by a court for a defendant convicted of a crime.

Sentencing guidelines: A set of rules and principles established by the United States Sentencing Commission that trial judges use to determine the sentence for a convicted defendant.

Testimony: Evidence presented orally by witnesses during trials or before grand juries.

Tort: A civil, not criminal, wrong. A negligent or intentional injury against a person or property, apart from breach of contract.

U.S. Attorney: A lawyer appointed by the President in each judicial district to prosecute and defend cases for the federal government. The U.S. Attorney employs a staff of Assistant U.S. Attorneys who appear as the government's attorneys in individual cases.

Uphold: The appellate court agrees with the lower court decision and allows it to stand. See affirmed.

Venue: The geographic area in which a court has jurisdiction. A change of venue is a change or transfer of a case from judicial district to another.

Verdict: The decision of a trial jury or a judge that determines the guilt or innocence of a criminal defendant, or that determines the final outcome of a civil case.

Warrant: Court authorization, most often for law enforcement officers, to conduct a search or make an arrest.

Witness: A person called upon by either side in a lawsuit to give testimony before the court or jury.

Writ: A written court order directing a person to take, or refrain from taking, a certain act.

Writ of certiorari: An order issued by the U.S. Supreme Court directing the lower court to transmit records for a case which it will hear on appeal.

For additional terms see: uscourts.gov/glossary.

Raymond E. Lumsden

About the Author

Raymond Lumsden is currently an inmate in the Texas Department of Criminal Justice, where he continues to fight his wrongful conviction.

He has more than 30 years of legal experience in family law, criminal law, civil legislation and appellate law. Combining that experience with his advanced training and certifications in legal writing, he has accounted for hundreds of motions, writs and petitions being granted relief on behalf of himself and others.

He is the father of four children and the grandfather of three. Currently he is pursuing his Juris Doctorate through a correspondence program.

Raymond has authored dozens of books such as, *The Pro Se Section 1983 Manual*; *The Habeas Corpus Manual*; *Ask, Believe, Receive*, etc.

Raymond E. Lumsden

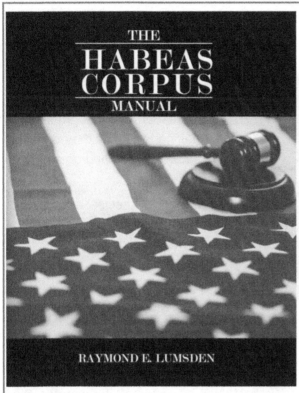

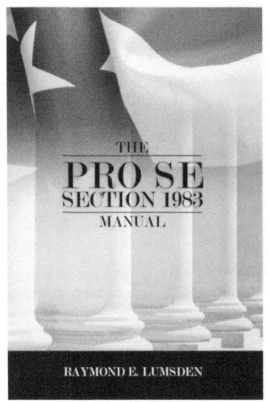

FREEBIRD PUBLISHERS, Box 541, North Dighton, MA 02764   www.freebirdpublishers.com

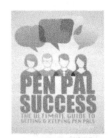

Raymond E. Lumsden

 # Freebird Publishers
Post-Conviction Relief Series

Post-Conviction Relief Books

⇒ Secrets Exposed

⇒ The Appeal

⇒ Advancing Your Claim

⇒ Winning Claims

⇒ C.O.A. in the Supreme Court

Coming Soon

Post-Conviction Relief: Second Last Chance

Post-Conviction Relief: The Advocate

Each Only
$26.99
Includes S/H
with tracking

Post-Conviction Relief is a subject most often pursued only by prisoners, the people who are most deprived of the necessary information. What is offered in most law libraries, is in inadequate, because what is needed is watered down by piles of useless and confusing information. That's why the Post-Conviction Relief series was written. It is a no-nonsense guide, to legal research, that is written in a language that anyone can understand. Most importantly, each book has been written to serve a specific purpose, as instructions for a specific step in the Post-Conviction process. With this collection of books, the average person can quickly become a more powerful advocate than they have ever been before, even if only on their own case. Within this set of books, the reader will find that there is something for all prisoners, whether it's their first day in prison or their first day of supervised release.

★ The best instruction one can receive is the words of experience. The Post-Conviction Relief series is written by a real advocate who has actually been there and prevailed in many cases.

★ In most cases prisoners have only one year to make their claims, the Post-Conviction Relief series is the no-nonsense path to understanding the process.

★ The Post-Conviction Relief series provides its readers with the court rules that pertain to Post Conviction Relief. A great resource for prisoners who are often locked down.

★ Post-Conviction Relief: you want to succeed, follow my lead.

★ All books are not created equal. Get only what you need with the Post-Conviction Relief series.

All Books Softcover, 8x10", B&W, 190+ pages EACH $26.99 includes s/h with tracking

Written in simple terms for everyone to understand, it's not just for lawyers anymore.

NO ORDER FORM NEEDED CLEARLY WRITE ON PAPER & SEND PAYMENT TO:

Freebird Publishers Box 541, North Dighton, MA 02764

Diane@FreebirdPublishers.com   www.FreebirdPublishers.com

Toll Free: 888-712-1987   Text/Phone: 774-406-8682

amazon.com

Thanks for your interest in
Freebird Publishers!

We value our customers and would love to hear from you! Reviews are an important part in bringing you quality publications. We love hearing from our readers-rather it's good or bad (though we strive for the best)!

If you could take the time to review/rate any publication you've purchased with Freebird Publishers we would appreciate it!

If your loved one uses Amazon, have them post your review on the books you've read. This will help us tremendously, in providing future publications that are even more useful to our readers and growing our business.

Amazon works off of a 5 star rating system. When having your loved one rate us be sure to give them your chosen star number as well as a written review. Though written reviews aren't required, we truly appreciate hearing from you.

☆ ☆ ☆ ☆ ☆ **Everything a prisoner needs is available in this book.**
January 30, 201 June 7, 2018
Format: Paperback

A necessary reference book for anyone in prison today. This book has everything an inmate needs to keep in touch with the outside world on their own from inside their prison cell. Inmate Shopper's business directory provides complete contact information on hundreds of resources for inmate services and rates the companies listed too! The book has even more to offer, contains numerous sections that have everything from educational, criminal justice, reentry, LGBT, entertainment, sports schedules and more. The best thing is each issue has all new content and updates to keep the inmate informed on todays changes. We recommend everybody that knows anyone in prison to send them a copy, they will thank you.

* No purchase neccessary. Reviews are not required for drawing entry. Void where prohibited.
  Contest date runs July 1 - June 30, 2019.

Made in United States
Orlando, FL
12 February 2025